LOVE FOR THE MESSENGER

MUHAMMAD ﷺ

LOVE FOR THE MESSENGER MUHAMMAD ﷺ

MUḤADDITH AL-SHĀM

Shaykh Nūr al-Dīn ʿItr

TRANSLATED & ANNOTATED BY

Usman Ali

Love for the Messenger Muhammad ﷺ

Published by: Heritage Press
Website: www.heritagepress.co.uk
E-mail: info@heritagepress.co.uk

Author: Shaykh Nūr al-Dīn ʿItr
Translated by: Usman Ali

A CIP catalogue record of this book is available from the British Library.

ISBN 978-0-8382479-0-4

Typeset & Cover by: nqaddoura@hotmail.com
Printed by: TJ Books, UK

In the words of Ḥassān ibn Thābit ﷺ, the poet
of the Messenger of Allah ﷺ, who said:

'Better than you, my eye has never seen,

And more beautiful than you, the women
have never given birth,

You were created free of any defect,

It is as though you were created as you so desired.'

Dear Reader

An earnest request is made to your gracious self to recite the opening chapter of the Qur'an, the *Fātiḥah*, each time you begin to read from this book, and dedicate its reward to our master, the greatest of creation and the Seal of all Prophets, the Messenger of Allah, Muhammad ﷺ. And thereafter to the Teacher to the Scholars, the great gnostic and hadith master of Greater Syria, the late al-Sayyid Shaykh Nūr al-Dīn ʿItr رحمه الله, and his beloved, exemplary and scholarly son, the late Dr. Muḥammad Mujāhid رحمه الله. May Allah reward him ﷺ, his family and those that taught us their way with the greatest of rewards! Āmīn!

Contents

Transliteration Key | xii
Translator's Introduction | xiii
Author's Biography | xviii
Introduction | 1

PART ONE
Defining the Love of the Messenger ﷺ

Preamble | 5
Motives for loving | 7
Love of perfection | 8
Love of immense generosity | 10
Love of Allah and His Messenger ﷺ is above all else | 12
The various forms of love | 14
The role of reflection | 15
The reality of love | 18
Compulsory love | 19
Sunnah love | 20

PART TWO

RECOGNISING AND INSTILLING LOVE OF THE MESSENGER ﷺ

Indicative signs and factors engendering love | 25

Emulating the Messenger of Allah ﷺ | 26

Love of the noble Qur'an | 27

Love for his sunnah & reading his words ﷺ | 29

Love of his biography & characteristics ﷺ | 30

Profusely mentioning him & revering him whenever he is mentioned ﷺ | 31

Profusely yearning to meet him ﷺ | 33

Profusely invoking blessings and peace upon him ﷺ | 35

PART THREE

THE LOVE OF THE COMMUNITY OF THE COMPANIONS ﷻ AS A WHOLE

The love of all the Companions ﷻ for the Prophet ﷺ | 39

Love during the Battle of Badr | 41

Love during the Battle of al-Rajīᶜ | 43

Love during the Battle of Banū Muṣṭaliq | 45

Love during the threat of war at Ḥudaybiyyah | 47

Loving Allah and His Messenger ﷺ & acquiring their love in return | 50

The Battle of Ḥunayn and the love of the Anṣār | 52

The Companions vying in the love of the Messenger of Allah ﷺ | 56

The Companions' feelings of love for the Messenger ﷺ | 58

PART FOUR

THE LOVE OF THE FOUR RIGHTLY GUIDED CALIPHS FOR THE MESSENGER ﷺ

Abū Bakr the Veracious' love ؓ | 63

ʿUmar ibn al-Khaṭṭāb's love ؓ | 69

ʿUthmān ibn ʿAffān's love ؓ | 74

ʿAlī ibn Abī Ṭālib's love ؓ | 81

PART FIVE

NOTABLE INSTANCES OF THE COMPANIONS' LOVE FOR THE MESSENGER ﷺ

Abū Ayyūb al-Anṣārī's hospitality ؓ | 89

Sawād ibn al-Ghaziyyah ؓ kissing the Prophet's abdomen ﷺ | 91

Umm ʿAmmārah ؓ sacrificing herself for the Prophet ﷺ | 93

Seeking solace with the Prophet ﷺ during great calamities | 95

Yearning for the Messenger of Allah ﷺ | 98

PART SIX

CONCLUSION

The hallmarks of true love for the Messenger ﷺ | 103

Concluding remarks | 106

TRANSLITERATION KEY

ء ʾ (A distinctive glottal stop made at the bottom of the throat.)

ا *a*, *ā*

ب *b*

ت *t*

ث *th* (Pronounced like the *th* in *think*.)

ج *j*

ح *ḥ* (Hard *h* sound made at the Adam's apple in the middle of the throat.)

خ *kh* (Pronounced like the *ch* in Scottish *loch*.)

د *d*

ذ *dh* (Pronounced like the *th* in *this*.)

ر *r*

س *s*

ش *sh*

ص *ṣ* (An emphatic *s* pronounced behind the upper front teeth.)

ض *ḍ* (An emphatic *d*-like sound made by pressing the entire tongue against the upper palate.)

ط *ṭ* (An emphatic *t* pronounced behind the front teeth.)

ظ *ẓ* (An emphatic *th*, like the *th* in *this*, made behind the front teeth.)

ع ʿ (A distinctive Semitic sound made in the middle of the throat, sounding to a Western ear more like a vowel than a consonant.)

غ *gh* (A guttural sound made at the top of the throat, resembling the untrilled German and French *r*.)

ف *f*

ق *q* (A guttural *k* sound produced at the back of the palate.)

ك *k*

ل *l*

م *m*

ن *n*

ه *h*

و *w*, *u*, *ū*

ي *y*, *i*, *ī*

Translator's Introduction

In the name of Allah, the Lord of the Worlds, and may the best of blessings and the most perfect of greetings be upon our master Muhammad ﷺ, his family, Companions and those who follow them with excellence until the final hour.

Allah Most High said, 'Say: If it be that your fathers, your sons, your brothers, your spouses, or your kindred, the wealth that you have gained, the commerce in which you fear a decline, or the dwellings in which you delight are dearer to you than Allah, or His Messenger, or the striving in His cause, then wait until Allah brings about His decision! Allah guides not the rebellious.'[1] With that, Allah Most High ruled one who held the beloved things of men dearer than Allah and His Messenger ﷺ to be a rebellious slave and promised His chastisement against him. By mentioning the Messenger ﷺ alongside His own name in the verse, Allah thereby emphasised the importance of the love of the Messenger ﷺ.

He Most High also stated, 'The Prophet has greater right over the believers than [they have for] themselves.'[2] These verses and numerous others

1 Qur'an 9:24.
2 Qur'an 33:6.

highlight the essential need to expand on the subject of loving the Messenger of Allah ﷺ and clarify its absolute obligation upon all Muslims.

None displayed more love for Allah and His Messenger than the Companions of the Elect Prophet ﷺ. Those who strove with their might and sacrificed their lives for Allah and His Messenger.

The Commander of the Faithful ʿAlī ؓ was once asked, 'What was your (i.e. the Companions') love for the Messenger of Allah ﷺ like?' To which he replied, 'The Messenger of Allah ﷺ was more beloved to us than our wealth, children, fathers, mothers and more beloved to us than cool water at the point of thirst.'

His statement showed that the Companions ؓ had encapsulated the meaning of the Prophet's words ﷺ, 'None of you [truly] believes until I am more beloved to him than his father, his child and the whole of mankind.' They truly were as Allah had described in the Qur'an, 'That is because neither thirst nor toil nor hunger afflicts them in the way of Allah, nor do they take any step that raises the ire of the disbelievers, nor gain they any gain from the enemy, but it was reckoned to their credit as a deed of righteousness. For Allah loses not the reward of those who do good.'[3]

The current work is the second rendition into English of the Arabic treatise entitled *Ḥubb al-rasūl ṣallallāhu ʿalayhi wa ālihi wa ṣaḥbihi wa sallama min al-īmān* [Loving the Messenger ﷺ is a part of faith], which was authored by the leading hadith authority of Greater Syria (*Muḥaddith al-Shām*) – the erudite scholar and teacher to the scholars – my master Shaykh Nūr al-Dīn ʿItr ؒ.

3 Qur'an 9:120.

I was very fortunate to have been hosted as a guest by Shaykh Nūr al-Dīn ʿItr ﷺ at his Damascus home in 2010, when I was gifted a copy of the present work among others. He subtly intimated that some of the works I was gifted should be translated. I am eternally grateful to Allah for the ability to fulfil his subtle request by presenting this translation of his work. The second of the works gifted was translated and published in 2019, entitled *Muhammad, Messenger to Mankind* ﷺ. I present this work to the Muslim reader, intending to fulfil the Shaykh's wish in part and hoping that in the near future – if Allah wills – I may complete his wish by translating the third treatise he had gifted me, entitled *Ittibāʿ al-rasūl ṣallallāhu ʿalayhi wa sallama min al-īmān,* [Emulating the Messenger ﷺ is a part of faith].

Unfortunately, during the production of this book we received the sad news that our beloved shaykh had passed away following his battle with Parkinson's disease. We ask Allah to envelop him with His Mercy, grant him a lofty station in the hereafter and reward him generously on our behalf. Āmīn.

The present work defines what sincere love of the Messenger ﷺ is, and the means by which one may acquire it, and increase in it. It acquaints the reader with the hallmarks of true love for the Messenger ﷺ as exemplified by the best generation of Muslims, the Companions of the one sent as 'a mercy to the worlds.'[4] The examples of the Companions' conduct during his life ﷺ, which are enumerated in this work, provide a lucid account of utmost love, sincerity and devotion to Allah and the Messenger ﷺ.

The translation has been revised for this second rendition and numerous footnotes have been added to clarify subtle themes. Definitions of technical terms, descriptions of locations and short biographies of figures who

4 Qur'an 21:107.

may be unfamiliar to the reader have been provided where appropriate. All Qur'anic quotations have been cited in the footnotes. The author's footnotes are marked by [A] and all others are those of the translator. Where deemed necessary, some of the author's explanatory footnotes have been incorporated into the body of the text.

I would like to thank Shaykh Amjad Mahmood for his help in reviewing the translation, Rumeana Jahangir for copyediting the work and Naeim Qaddoura for typesetting and cover design. I would also like to extend my gratitude to my good friends Ustadh Rashid Khan, Khabir Mahmood and Usman Malik for their help in proofreading and refining the text. May Allah reward them all generously and grant them the very best in this life and the one to come.

Imam Muslim narrated that Rabīᶜah ibn Kaᶜb al-Aslamī ؓ said, 'I used to spend the night at the house of the Messenger of Allah ﷺ and bring him water for ablution and [tend to] any other need. So one day he said to me, "Ask [for what you desire]," and I replied, "O Messenger of Allah ﷺ, I ask for your company in heaven." Thereupon he ﷺ said, "Or would you prefer something else?" So I replied, "That is all." He ﷺ said, "Then assist me in helping you, through much prostration".'

Ibn Abī Shaybah narrates on the authority of Abū ᶜUbaydah ؓ that ᶜAbd-Allāh ibn Masᶜūd ؓ was asked, "What was the supplication you made the night when the Messenger of Allah ﷺ said to you, 'Ask and you shall be given'." Ibn Masᶜūd replied, "I said, 'O Allah I ask you for faith that does not waver, joy that never ceases and the company of your Prophet ﷺ in the highest station of paradise – the eternal garden'."'

Truly the Companions were, as the 19th century philosopher and historian Thomas Carlyle expressed, 'They called him Prophet, you say?

Why, he stood there, face to face with them; bare, not enshrined in any mystery; visibly clouting his own cloak, cobbling his own shoes; fighting, counselling, ordering in the midst of them: they must have seen what kind of a man he was, let him be called what you like! No emperor with his tiaras was obeyed as this man in a cloak of his own clouting. During three-and-twenty years of rough actual trial. I find something of a veritable Hero necessary for that, of itself.'[5]

5 Carlyle, Thomas, *On heroes, hero-worship and the heroic in history*.

Author's Biography

Muḥaddith al-Shām
Shaykh Nūr al-Dīn ʿItr

He is the venerable, erudite scholar, hadith master and meticulous researcher, the remnant of the way of the righteous predecessors, the teacher, Shaykh Dr. Nūr al-Dīn Muḥammad ibn Ḥasan ʿItr al-Ḥalabī. His lineage returns to our Master al-Ḥasan ibn ʿAlī . While his mother – may Allah envelop her with His Mercy – is the daughter of the erudite scholar and gnostic Shaykh Muḥammad Najīb Sirāj al-Dīn al-Ḥusaynī . Thus Shaykh Nūr al-Dīn ʿItr is a descendent of al-Ḥasan with respect to his father and a descendant of al-Ḥusayn with respect to his mother. Owing to the shaykh's humility, his lofty lineage and ascription to the Prophet is not to be found upon the sixty or so books he has published over the years.

He was born in the city of Aleppo al-Shahbā', Syria on Wednesday 17 Ṣafar, 1356 AH corresponding to 28 April 1937. He was brought up and flourished in a religious and pure scholastic household. His primary education was at the Sayf al-Dawlah Madrasa before moving on to the Khusrawiyyah School, where he was introduced to the eminent scholar Shaykh Rābigh al-Ṭabbākh , with whom he studied hadith. He later graduated with a diploma with distinction in Shariah from the school. In his formative years, he also attended the public lessons of his grandfather, the gnostic of Aleppo ʿAllāmah Shaykh Muḥammad Najīb Sirāj al-Dīn.

The most influential of all his teachers was his maternal uncle, the late erudite hadith master of Aleppo Shaykh ʿAbd-Allāh Sirāj al-Dīn al-Ḥusaynī, attending many of his lessons and studying under his tutelage. He benefitted greatly both from his deep knowledge of the science of hadith as well as his profound spiritual state. Shaykh Nūr al-Dīn would later author a biography in his uncle's remembrance entitled, *Ṣafaḥāt min ḥayāt al-imām shaykh al-islām ʿabd-allāh sirāj al-dīn*, [Pages from the life of the Imam Shaykh al-Islam ʿAbd-Allāh Sirāj al-Dīn].

Among the scholars with whom he studied in Aleppo were: Shaykh ʿAbd al-Wahhāb al-Sukkar, Shaykh Muḥammad al-Salqīnī, Shaykh Muḥammad Najīb Khayyāṭah, Shaykh Muḥammad Abū al-Khayr Zayn al-ʿĀbidīn, Shaykh Bakrī Rajab and others. He obtained a bachelor's degree from the faculty of Shariah at the University of al-Azhar, where he was also awarded an international certificate with distinction, at the level of professorship from the department of Qur'anic exegesis and hadith.

During his time at al-Azhar, he studied with some of the greatest luminaries of the age, such as the great researcher and scholar Shaykh Muḥammad Muḥyī al-Dīn ʿAbd al-Ḥamīd. The latter was his primary supervisor for his doctorate, with whom he also studied the science of hadith from al-Suyūṭī's *Tadrīb al-rāwī sharḥ taqrīb al-nawāwī.*

Among the scholars with whom he developed a strong connection, was Shaykh Muṣṭafā Mujāhid, whom he described as, 'A jurist that was open about the truth, not fearing the blame of any critic regarding Allah.' Regarding him he stated, 'He was like a father to me, he would specifically ask about my studies and personal life.' As a result of his close connection to the shaykh, he named his first son Muḥammad Mujāhid after him.

He held many prestigious posts including: head of the department of Qur'anic exegesis and hadith in the faculty of Shariah, University of Damascus; head and professor of the department of Qur'anic exegesis and hadith, University Wing at the Institute of Shariah learning, Aleppo, and the Fatḥ Islamic Institute, Damascus; head of the faculty of Qur'anic exegesis and its sciences for higher education and head of the department of hadith for advanced studies at Abū Nūr Academy, Damascus. He continued to supervise MA and PhD students in Syria and other Arab states through to his advanced years.

Shaykh Nūr al-Dīn won both the first and second prizes at competitions in hadith studies that were organised by the Arab organisation for culture, education and science and participated in many national and international seminars and conferences. He lectured at the faculties of Shariah and fundamentals of religion at various universities including; Umm al-Qurā, Muḥammad ibn Saʿūd and, Imam Awzāʿī, as well as in Kuwait, Dubai, Algeria, alongside Marmarah University in Istanbul and numerous universities in India.

He was the lead editor for many scholarly journals in Saudi Arabia, Kuwait, Dubai, Lebanon, Syria, Jordan and Palestine. He also published many of his own articles and was the longstanding editor for the *Islamic Encyclopaedia*, Kuwait.

He authored more than fifty scholarly books and critical editions of classical works including: *Minhāj al-naqd fī ʿulūm al-ḥadīth* [The methodology of criticism in hadith sciences], *Imām al-tirmidhī wa muwāzanah bayna jāmiʿihi wa ṣaḥīḥayn* [Imam al-Tirmidhī and the comparison between his

Compendium and the *Ṣaḥīḥayn*], *Muʿjam al-muṣṭalaḥāt al-ḥadīthiyyah* [The dictionary of hadith terms], *ʿUlūm al-qur'ān al-karīm* [The sciences of the noble Qur'an], *Uṣūl al-jarḥ wa al-taʿdīl* [The principles of criticism and endorsement (of hadith narrators)], *al-Ḥajj wa al-ʿumrah fī al-fiqh al-islāmī* [Hajj and umrah in Islamic shariah], *ʿUlūm al-ḥadīth* [The sciences of hadith by Ibn al-Ṣalāḥ], *al-Riḥlah li ṭalab al-ḥadīth* [Journeying in pursuit of hadith by al-Baghdādī], *Sharḥ ʿilal al-tirmidhī* [The commentary on *al-Tirmidhī's* introduction to subtle discrepancies by Ibn Rajab al-Ḥanbalī], *al-Mughnī fī al-ḍuʿafā'* [The sufficient compendium of weak narrators by al-Dhahabī], *Nuzhah al-naẓar fī tawḍīḥ nukhbah al-fikr* [The pleasure of the gaze in exposition of select thought by Ibn Ḥajar], *Irshād ṭullāb al-ḥaqā'iq* [Guiding the seekers of truths by al-Nawawī], *Manāhij al-muḥaddithīn* [The methodologies of the hadith specialists], *Mādhā ʿan al-mar'ah* [What about women?], *Fikr al-muslim wa taḥiddiyāt al-alf al-thālithah* [Muslim thought and the challenges of the third millennium] and his acclaimed magnum opus *Iʿlām al-anām* [Announcement to mankind], a commentary upon al-Ḥāfiẓ Ibn Ḥajar's famed hadith collection *Bulūgh al-marām.*

He returned to his Lord on Wednesday 23 September, 2020 following a battle with Parkinson's disease in his later years. May Allah reward him generously and grant him a lofty station in the eternal garden. *Amīn.*

In the Name of Allah, the Merciful, the Compassionate

Introduction

All praise belongs to Allah, the Generous, the Benefactor, and may the greatest of blessings and greetings of peace be upon the greatest of creation – the most perfect of them all – our master Muhammad, his family, Companions and those that follow them with excellence through every age.

Truly loving the Prophet ﷺ is a tremendous method for the realisation of virtues and perfections. In fact, loving him ﷺ is a part of faith; and moreover, if it was not for him ﷺ, surely faith would never have been truly known.

This concise epistle acquaints the reader with the reality of this love and its practical application among the first generation of Muslims – the best of all generations. Providing a conceptual and practical representation of their love facilitates both the acquisition of this bounty and the realisation of this lofty station, resulting in the attainment of his glad tidings, for he ﷺ said: 'A person will be with whomever he loves.'

I chose a title for this work from a section of the Chapter of Faith, from Imam al-Bukhārī's *Ṣaḥīḥ*[6] entitled: 'Loving the Messenger ﷺ is a part of

6 The name commonly used to refer to the hadith collection of Imam al-Bukhāri and generally accepted to be the most rigorously authenticated of all the hadith collections.

faith.' In a similar manner, I too have compiled narrations on the topic that are established to be rigorously-authenticated[7]. With this latter comment I suffice myself from extensive referencing and analysis of their chains of transmission, except in certain instances, where I mention their verification as being authentic for extra emphasis. Hence all contents of this treatise, by the grace of Allah are substantiated and accepted.

O Allah, establish within us the love about which our master Muhammad ﷺ said, 'A person will be with whomever he loves.' *Āmīn.*

7 'The rigorously-authenticated (*ṣaḥīḥ*) hadith is an unbroken hadith whose chain of narration is completely connected [to the primary source], with transmission by [individuals of] uprightness – one after the other up until its very end and it is neither anomalous nor defective [...] and neither is there any objectionable defect nor any type of criticism aimed at any of its narrators.' Ibn al-Ṣalāḥ, al-Ḥāfiẓ ʿUthmān ibn ʿAbd al-Raḥmān al-Shahrazūrī, *Maʿrifah anwāʿ ʿulūm al-ḥadīth.*

PART ONE

DEFINING THE LOVE OF THE MESSENGER ﷺ

Preamble

Ḥubb and *Maḥabbah* are two Arabic expressions used for love, an emotion held in the heart that is the most accommodating and compelling of attributes, for it is the inclination of the heart towards an object of affection. This emotion inscribes upon the individual certain feelings and instils behaviours whereby the lover sacrifices everything, both expensive and inexpensive, for the sake of pleasing his beloved. What's more, the lover becomes oblivious to his own self, in a passion for his beloved, and his own characteristics transform to those of his beloved.

There is no doubt that Allah Most High – the Lord of the Universe and its Creator – is most worthy of every expression of love and to the greatest degree, for indeed He holds the attributes of perfection, those that are infinite and innumerable. Similarly, He is the One who, from the treasures of His grace, pours countless blessings and limitless favours upon His Servants. 'And if you [try to] count the blessings of Allah, you will not [be able] to exhaust them.'[8] Truly they cannot be enumerated, except for a few, and only a small segment of their vastness can truly be understood, as indicated by the verse, 'You will not [be able] to exhaust them.'

8 Qur'an 16:18.

Our prophet and master Muhammad – may Allah bless him, his family and Companions and grant them peace – is the most deserving of all creation to be loved. Furthermore he is more deserving of your love than even your own self. Allah Most High stated, 'The Prophet has greater right over the believers than [they have for] themselves, and his wives are [like] their mothers.'[9] This verse has given him priority over yourself, and thus it includes every object of love. Contemplate and ponder over this comment, 'The Prophet has greater right over the believers than [they have for] themselves.'

9 Qur'an 33:6.

The Motives for Loving

Whoever knows the Messenger of Allah ﷺ, knows the reality of such love. In fact, he experiences it, for the traits that cause the believer to have love for him ﷺ have been perfected and do not exist in any other creation. The imams of scholarship, gnosis and love have summarised the reasons according to two principle categories – the perfect qualities demonstrated in his character and his generosity.

LOVE OF PERFECTION

In this case, the lover loves another for his beautiful form, pleasant voice or some other aspect of beauty. The Prophet ﷺ has surpassed all of creation both in physical beauty and form, as has been definitively mass-transmitted[10] from the Companions ؓ:

'The Messenger of Allah ﷺ was the most handsome of all people, and the finest of them in [physical] form.'

Hind ibn Abī Hālah ؓ stated, 'The Messenger of Allah was grand and majestic, and his face shone like the moon on the night of the full moon.' Abū Hurayrah ؓ stated, 'I have not seen anyone more beautiful than the Messenger of Allah ﷺ. It was as though the sun coursed through his face.'

Anas ibn Mālik ؓ stated, 'I have not touched silk brocade nor silken wares softer than the palm of the Messenger of Allah ﷺ. Nor have I smelt

---

10 '*Al-Mutawātir*: a report that is established upon the tongues of a people, [to the extent] that it is not conceivable that they colluded to forge a lie, owing to their quantity or for their uprightness. As is the case for when the Prophet ﷺ had claimed prophethood and a miracle was produced at his hands.' Al-Jurjānī, al-Sharīf ʿAlī ibn Muḥammad ibn ʿAlī al-Ḥusaynī, *Kitāb al-taʿrīfāt*.

musk or amber more fragrant than the scent of the Prophet ﷺ.' In another narration, he stated, '[Nor] more fragrant than the perspiration of the Messenger of Allah ﷺ.'

Truly, anyone who described him would say, 'I have not seen anyone before him nor after like him ﷺ.'

Therefore no matter how much you love the beauty of creation, it behoves you to love the Messenger of Allah ﷺ more so and more than your own self, for truly he was greater, more majestic and superior in beauty than every other beautiful thing.

The astute individual loves another for his excellent character and praiseworthy conduct, even if he is distant from him. So know that our Prophet Muhammad ﷺ was the most perfect of mankind in character. It suffices you to know the testimony of Allah Most High regarding him, 'Indeed, you stand above an outstanding standard of character.'[11] Reflect upon Allah's Words, 'above an outstanding standard of character,' to truly realise that there is no good character trait, nor perfection of a trait or soul, except that he ﷺ surpasses it, because the preposition 'above' demonstrates transcendence.

11 Qur'an 68:4.

Love of Exceptional Generosity

A person loves someone who grants him some good in this world whether it be once or twice. Yet no matter how large such a gift may be, it is finite and inevitably dissipates. In addition, a person will love someone who rescues him from something life-threatening or harmful, but that too comes to an end and does not endure. So how about this generous Prophet and magnificent Messenger, who has combined excellent character traits and generosity, and who grants you extensive gifts and vast far-reaching blessings? For through him, Allah Most High has removed us from the darkness of disbelief into the light of faith, and has rescued us from the fire of ignorance, so that we may enter gardens of certainty and gnosis.

Consider this well, so that you come to realise that he ﷺ is the cause of your everlasting existence in eternal bliss. So which benevolence is greater and more bountiful than his benevolence ﷺ towards you? How do we arise to show some gratitude to the Messenger ﷺ? Or fulfil his right over us, when, through him ﷺ our Lord has bestowed upon us the gifts of this world and the hereafter, and through him, Allah has showered upon us His Blessings, both hidden and apparent? Consequently, the Messenger

ﷺ has a right that you love him more than you love yourself, your family, offspring and the whole of mankind. The people of gnosis have stated, 'If in every hair follicle there was complete love for him ﷺ, truly that would only be part of what he ﷺ is deserving of.'

Love of Allah and His Messenger ﷺ is Above all Else

He Most High said, 'The Prophet has greater right over the believers than they have for themselves.'[12]

Furthermore the Almighty said, 'Say: If it be that your fathers, sons, brothers, wives or kindred; the wealth that you have gained; the commerce in which you fear a decline; or the dwellings in which you delight are dearer to you than Allah and His Messenger, or striving in His way, then wait until Allah brings about His command; and Allah does not guide the rebellious.'[13] This noble verse has gathered the various objects of love and made it incumbent that the love of Allah and His Messenger be preferred over each and every one of them, and preferred over all of them collectively.

With regards to that, there are hadiths that have been established with the utmost authenticity, as have been narrated in the Two Authentic Hadith

12 Qur'an 33:6.
13 Qur'an 9:24.

Collections[14] from Anas ibn Mālik ﷺ, that the Messenger of Allah ﷺ said, 'None of you [truly] believes until I am more beloved to him than his father, his son and the whole of mankind.' This encompasses all objects of love, and among them is your love for yourself due to his statement, 'and the whole of mankind.'

Al-Bukhārī and others narrated from Abū Hurayrah ﷺ that he stated, 'The Messenger of Allah ﷺ said, "By the One in whose hand is my soul, none of you [truly] believes until I am more beloved to him than his father and son".' He mentioned the father and the son, as they are the most beloved of things to man, and for their sake, he lives and strives in this world. Thus it suffices to mention these two, in place of all other objects of affection. In addition, he indicated that it is incumbent to give precedence to his love ﷺ over all other beloved and dear things, including one's self.

14 *Ṣaḥīḥayn*, literally 'The two *Ṣaḥīḥs*' the collective term for the two hadith collections entitled *Ṣaḥīḥ*, which were compiled by Imam al-Bukhārī and Imam Muslim respectively.

The Various Forms of Love

Among the best-known are the following:

1. Love borne out of compassion and mercy – the love of a father for his son.
2. Love borne out of veneration and respect – the love of a son for his father and a pupil for his teacher.
3. Instinctive love – the love of a man for his wife.
4. Love borne out of sincere concern and humanity – the love for the whole of mankind.
5. Love borne out of the ego – the love of man for himself, which is the strongest of all forms of love. It is a love that the self is naturally inclined to, just as it is inclined to other forms of love, though love borne out of ego is stronger than all other forms.

The Role of Reflection

Allah Most High and His Messenger ﷺ have emphasised that the love for them be greater in the heart of the believer than all other types of love. The way to attain this is by reflecting upon the things beloved to one while also contemplating upon the Messenger of Allah ﷺ. Here it is inevitable that the intellect, with its instinctual self-concern and its certainty in the virtues of the Messenger of Allah ﷺ, will prevail and leave behind no trace of any other object of affection.

O astute believer! You have an excellent example in our master ʿUmar ibn al-Khaṭṭāb ؓ. Imam al-Bukhārī narrated that ʿAbd-Allāh ibn Hishām ؓ said, 'We were with the Prophet ﷺ when he took the hand of ʿUmar ibn al-Khaṭṭāb. Whereupon ʿUmar said to him, "O Messenger of Allah, certainly you are more beloved to me than all things besides myself." The Prophet ﷺ replied, "No, by the One in whose hand is my soul, [your faith is not complete] until I become more beloved to you than your own self." So ʿUmar said to him, "By Allah, it is now the case that you are truly more beloved to me than my own self!" Thereupon the Prophet ﷺ said, "Now, O ʿUmar".'

The initial response of our master ʿUmar ؓ was a result of the natural inclinations of man. Then he pondered over what the Prophet ﷺ had said to him, 'No – i.e. your faith is not perfect – by the One in whose hand is my soul, until I become more beloved to you than your own self.' ʿUmar realised that the Prophet ﷺ was surely more beloved to him than his own self, for he ﷺ was the cause of ʿUmar's salvation from destruction in this life and the next. So he informed the Prophet ﷺ of his insight, reinforcing it with an oath: 'By Allah, it is now the case that you are truly more beloved to me than my own self!' To which he received the noble response, 'Now, O ʿUmar,' meaning now you have truly come to know and realise what is incumbent.

Thus contemplation leads you to the Messenger of Allah ﷺ being the most beloved, for when you look attentively, you will realise that the cause for the everlasting survival of your soul in eternal bliss is none other than the Messenger of Allah ﷺ and this benefit is the greatest good and source of blessings to you. Consequently, the Prophet ﷺ necessarily deserves that his share of your love surpasses that of anything else, and greater than even the soul that resides between your two sides. That is because the benefit and great good – the attainment of which kindles love – that you gain from him ﷺ is more than what you receive from anyone else and more than even your own self. Just as he ﷺ is the greatest man in terms of perfection and virtues, he is likewise the juncture at which the loftiest of perfections, virtues, divinely-bestowed blessings and good meet.

These emotions are preserved in the depths of the soul and embedded in the perception of the intellect, since every Muslim has love for Allah and His Messenger in his heart. For one does not enter Islam except by virtue of this love. However, people vary according to the extent of their recollection of the aforementioned emotions or their heedlessness of them. Accordingly, one of the greatest ways of calling to Allah is by celebrating the virtues and perfections of our master, the Messenger of Allah ﷺ. And to do so profusely in order to benefit oneself as well as other believers, to win the hearts of non-Muslims and attract them towards your true religion, and to reap one of the great fruits of loving him ﷺ – the sweetness of faith – regarding which the hadiths have been categorically established without any shadow of a doubt.

Al-Bukhārī and Muslim narrate on the authority of Anas ibn Mālik ؓ that the Prophet ﷺ said, 'Whoever has [these] three in him will find the sweetness of faith: that Allah and His Messenger are more beloved to him than anything besides them; that he loves an individual purely for the sake of Allah; and that he detests returning to disbelief just as he detests being cast into the Fire.'

Muslim narrated that al-ʿAbbās ibn ʿAbd al-Muṭṭalib ؓ heard the Messenger of Allah ﷺ say, 'Whoever is pleased with Allah as a Lord, Islam as a religion and with Muhammad ﷺ as a messenger, he has tasted the sweetness of faith.'

The Reality of Love

Know, O believer, that love is not a claim, nor mere wishful thinking. Rather, it is only demonstrated through carrying out the commands and avoiding the prohibitions [of the Sacred Law], and love, in this regard, is considered either compulsory[15] or sunnah[16].

15 *Farḍ*, 'That which is established by a decisive textual proof, with absolutely no doubt regarding it. Whoever denies it commits unbelief, and one who leaves it is punished for it.' Al-Jurjānī, al-Sharīf ʿAlī ibn Muḥammad ibn ʿAlī al-Ḥusaynī, *Kitāb al-taʿrīfāt*.

16 '*Al-Sunnah*, linguistically it is a way; whether it be pleasing to one or not. With regards to the Shariah, it is the way that is traversed in the religion without compulsion or obligation. Thus the sunnah is that which the Prophet ﷺ regularly maintained while occasionally leaving it. If the practice is in relation to worship, then it is regarded as part of the sunnahs of guidance (*sunan al-hudā*) and if it is in relation to habits then they are supplementary sunnahs (*sunan al-zawāʾid*). A sunnah of guidance is that whose establishment is perfection in the religion and that which, if left, entails offense or sin. A supplementary sunnah is a form of guidance if taken, i.e. their establishment are good deeds however, leaving them does not entail any offense nor sin.' Al-Jurjānī, al-Sharīf ʿAlī ibn Muḥammad ibn ʿAlī al-Ḥusaynī, *Kitāb al-taʿrīfāt*.

Compulsory Love

Compulsory love is that which moves the soul to undertake its obligations, to avoid sin, and to be content with what Allah Most High has ordained. Hence, whoever falls into disobedience by not conducting an obligation or by committing an unlawful act, has done so as a result of his shortcoming in love since he gave precedence to the whims of his ego. That is from heedlessness – may Allah Most High protect us!

SUNNAH LOVE

Sunnah love is that which causes one to persevere with supererogatory acts[17] and avoid falling into doubtful matters.[18] In short, the believer who loves the Messenger of Allah ﷺ only receives commands and prohibitions from the light of his prophetic lamp ﷺ, he treads no path besides that of the Prophet ﷺ and he has the utmost contentment with what the Messenger has legislated. Thus he moulds his character in line with the Prophet's character ﷺ. Nor does the believer find any constraint within himself regarding that which he has judged to be the case. Thus

---

17 *Nawāfil*: 'In the sacred law it is considered to be that which has been legislated in excess of compulsory and obligatory acts and it has also been termed *mandūb*, *mustaḥabb* and *al-taṭawwuʿ*.' Al-Jurjānī, al-Sharīf ʿAlī ibn Muḥammad ibn ʿAlī al-Ḥusaynī, *Kitāb al-taʿrīfāt*.

18 *Shubuhāt* are doubtful matters, i.e. where there is doubt and obscurity over their permissibility, which have not been conclusively ruled upon. It is mentioned in the hadith of al-Bukhārī, on the authority of Abū ʿAbd-Allāh al-Nuʿmān ibn Bashīr ؓ, who stated, 'I heard the Messenger of Allah ﷺ, say, "Indeed the lawful is clear and the unlawful is clear, and between them are doubtful matters that many people do not know. Therefore, whoever avoids the doubtful matters (*shubuhāt*) has cleansed his religion and his honour and whoever falls into doubtful matters, falls into that which is unlawful; just like the shepherd who pastures [his flock] around a sanctuary is on the verge of pasturing [his flock] in it. Verily every king has a sanctuary and Allah's Sanctuary is His Prohibitions".'

whoever strives against his self in order to achieve this state will discover the sweetness of faith.

Al-Bukhārī narrates that Abū Hurayrah ﷺ said, 'The Messenger of Allah ﷺ said, "Allah Most High has stated, 'Whoever has enmity towards a Friend[19] of Mine, then I have declared war upon him. My Slave does not draw closer to Me with anything more beloved to Me than what I have made compulsory upon him; and My Slave continues to draw nearer to Me with supererogatory acts until I love him'."'

This hadith limits the causes of love to two – the performance of compulsory acts and the gaining of closeness to Allah through supererogatory acts. The lover does not cease to increase in supererogatory acts until he becomes beloved to Allah. Thus when the slave becomes beloved to Allah, the love of Allah Most High for him, will necessarily instil a second love within him for Allah – one that is greater than his initial love for Him. This gifted secondary love preoccupies the heart of the one seeking closeness from thinking or being concerned with anything other than his Beloved. Furthermore this love dominates the soul, such that the remembrance of the Beloved, his love for Him and his lofty ideals take control over the reins of his heart and prevails over his soul.

In summary, there is no praiseworthy, blissful life except through the love of Allah and His Messenger ﷺ. And there is no life except the life of the ardent lovers, those who find true joy in their beloved. Their souls are at peace with him, their hearts find tranquillity in him, they draw comfort in being close to him and delight in his love.

---

19 *Walī*: 'The *walī* is he who has gnosis of Allah and His Characteristics in accordance with that which is possible. He is persistent upon the acts of obedience and avoidance of acts of disobedience, and is one who abandons the engrossment with lusts and carnal desires.' Al-Jurjānī, al-Sharīf ʿAlī ibn Muḥammad ibn ʿAlī al-Ḥusaynī, *Kitāb al-taʿrīfāt*.

PART TWO

Recognising & Instilling Love of the Messenger ﷺ

Indicative Signs and Factors Engendering Love

Your love for the Prophet ﷺ is a precious stone, shining tremendously in the heart, whose rays will inevitably brighten with lights that illuminate it. These lights, which are manifestations of love, are also factors that increase and develop one's love, until one reaches the degree of being the beloved of both Allah Most High and His Messenger ﷺ. In fact, the point is not only for you to love Allah Most High and His Messenger ﷺ, rather the ultimate aim, success, achievement and supreme triumph is for Allah and His Messenger ﷺ to love you. O Allah, make us from among them!

We shall briefly present the most important of these signs that are indicative of love and factors that engender love. May Allah enable me and you to maintain them in their perfect degrees.

Emulating the Messenger of Allah ﷺ

Emulation is the greatest sign of love and the strongest factor in developing love. As for emulation being a sign, it is evident that a lover conforms to his beloved, otherwise he is a liar. As for it being a factor that engenders love, then such emulation enables a believer to experientially feel the beauty and perfection of what the Messenger of Allah ﷺ brought. This increases Allah and his Messenger's ﷺ love for the believer and proximity to him.

Allah has made the emulation of His Prophet ﷺ a test for the authenticity of one's claim to love Allah. Allah Most High said to the Prophet ﷺ, 'Say: "If you love Allah, then follow me. Allah will love you".'[20]

20 Qur'an 3:31.

Love of the Noble Qur'an

The Qur'an is the Speech of Allah, establishing the prophethood of our master Muhammad, the Messenger of Allah ﷺ. By means of it, the Prophet ﷺ guided creation to the truth and completely refined each characteristic,[21] until he became the greatest of creation in character. 'Indeed, you [stand] above an outstanding standard of character.' So test the love of the Qur'an in your heart and pleasure in listening to it – is it greater than the pleasure that people of music and vain desires experience in their listening? If so, then you are genuine in your love, for it is well known that whoever loves someone finds his words and speech to be the most cherished of things. So how about the Qur'an, which has surpassed the previously revealed Scriptures of Allah, both in their composition and content, and contains the manifestations of the Real[22] in its structure and

21 'Regarding the accumulation of the noble characteristics in him; he – upon him be peace – stated, in that which is narrated by al-Ṭabarānī in *al-Awsaṭ* on the authority of Jābir ؓ, "Indeed Allah sent me with all the noble character traits, perfection and the most beautiful of actions." In the narration of Mālik in the *Muwaṭṭa'*, "I was only sent to perfect noble character traits." Thus each and every praiseworthy characteristic is found in him ﷺ, for he was refined by the Qur'an.' Al-Nāblūsī, ʿAbd al-Ghanī ibn Ismāʿīl, *Al-Ḥadīqah al-nadiyyah.*

22 *Al-Ḥaqq*, the Real – one of the names of Allah.

depth? The beauty of its exposition and the perfection of its arrangement has made mankind and jinnkind unable to produce anything like it.

Allah has named the Qur'an 'a spirit,' as expressed in the following verse, 'Likewise we have revealed to you a spirit from our affair.'[23] Thus revelation is a spirit unto the souls, in the same way the soul is the life of bodies. How can a lover be satiated with the speech of his beloved, when it is meant to be his utmost desire to listen to it? May Allah be pleased with our master ʿUthmān ☙, for he said, 'Had our hearts been pure, they would not have been satiated with Allah's Speech.'

---

23 Qur'an 42:52.

Love for his Sunnah and Reading his Words ﷺ

One of the requirements of true love is for the lover to conform to his beloved. Therefore loving the Prophet ﷺ necessitates following his sunnah, i.e. his path. Whoever is unable to understand it, then let him ask a scholar who does.

Similarly, the words of the Messenger of Allah ﷺ are the words of the beloved, the best of mankind, and they are the best words man has ever uttered – beautiful in meaning and subtle in structure. If you do not reach that degree, then listen to them and attend gatherings wherein his words are read ﷺ, and observe where you stand in relation to these circles.

Love of his Biography and Characteristics ﷺ

It is natural for a lover to know his beloved. The Prophet's biography and his characteristics ﷺ acquaint you with the person of the noble Prophet ﷺ, upon him be the best of blessings and perfect salutations. Whenever your knowledge of him increases, your love for him grows, because your cognisance of his perfection has increased. Thus will you be granted perfection in love for him ﷺ, and his noble spirituality will prevail over your heart, such that Allah renders him ﷺ as your tutor, teacher, guide and exemplar. Just as Allah has made him His Prophet, Messenger and Chosen Guide ﷺ.

From this point of departure, it is necessary for a believer who loves him ﷺ to know his biography – his early life and how revelation was revealed to him, his qualities and mannerisms, his movements and moments of composure, his wakefulness and sleep, his worship of his Lord, his interactions with his family, his noble conduct with his Companions, and other than that of his affairs ﷺ, until it becomes as though one is present with him ﷺ, as one of his Companions.

Profusely Mentioning Him and Revering Him Whenever He is Mentioned ﷺ

Some of the gnostics have stated, 'Love is the constant remembrance of the beloved,' and the sages concur that someone who loves something mentions it profusely.

For example, in relation to revering the Prophet ﷺ is mentioning him with the honorific title of 'master'[24] and by displaying humility and

24 *Sayyid*: 'His words ﷺ, "I am the master of the children of Adam on the day of resurrection and the first whose grave will break open, the first to intercede and the first to be granted intercession." Al-Harawī stated, "The *sayyid* is he who has surpassed his people in good," while others have stated, "He is the one with whom refuge is sought during calamities and hardships. Thereupon he concerns himself with their affair, bears their adversities on their behalf and casts them away from them." As for his words ﷺ, "on the day of resurrection," this is in addition to him being their master in the life of this world also, as well as in the afterlife. The reason for specifying this is that, on the day of resurrection, his mastery will be clear to every individual and there shall not remain a single person to deny nor obstinately defy this, as opposed to the worldly life. For therein the sovereigns of the disbelievers and the claimants among the polytheists contest this. This is similar to the meaning of His Words Most High (40:16), "Who has sovereignty on the day that belongs to Allah, the One, the Subduer." For sovereignty also belongs to Him, transcendent is He, prior to that day. However, in the life of

submission when mentioning his noble name or hearing it. This was observed regarding many of the Companions and those after them.

An example of whom is our master Anas ibn Mālik ﷺ, who said, 'The Messenger of Allah ﷺ said one day...' and then he began to tremble and his clothes fluttered, and that was due to his reverence for the Messenger of Allah ﷺ. The hadith depicting the deep reverence shown by the Companions in the year of al-Ḥudaybiyyah[25] for the Messenger of Allah ﷺ, shall be discussed in the following section.

this world, there were those who claimed sovereignty or it was attributed to them metaphorically. Thus He restricted it all to the afterlife.' Al-Nawawī, Abū Zakariyyā Yaḥyā ibn Sharaf, *Al-Minhāj fī sharḥ saḥīḥ muslim ibn al-ḥajjāj*.

25 'In the sixth year after the migration, the peace treaty of al-Ḥudaybiyyah was established and the Prophet ﷺ agreed to a truce with the pagans for ten years. The Muslims thought it was a compromise with their enemies, while in reality it was a victory for them. Allah Most High said regarding it (48:1), "Indeed, We have made a great manifest opening for you." During this period, the souls fell into tranquil submission and the zeal for fighting and clashing abated. As a consequence, people became more inclined to listen to the call of Islam, and the Muslims enjoyed the freedom to travel and convey the call [to Islam] and the Qur'an. Thus the interest in Islam grew and a group of the seniors of Quraysh – amongst them Khālid ibn al-Walīd, ʿAmr ibn al-ʿĀṣ and ʿUthmān ibn Ṭalḥah – the gatekeeper of the noble Kaaba – accepted Islam.' ʿItr, Nūr al-Dīn, *al-Nafaḥāt al-ʿiṭriyyah*.

Profusely Yearning to Meet Him ﷺ

Every lover yearns to meet his beloved, so how must it be for the one who loves the Prophet ﷺ? He desires to see him in his dreams and meet him in person in the next life, to the extent that some of the gnostics stated, 'True love is [but] yearning for the beloved.'

Among the best-known examples of this profound yearning is when our master Bilāl ؓ[26] was on his deathbed and his wife due to her anguish

26 'Ibn ʿAsākir relates with a good chain of narration – as stated by al-Ḥāfiẓ al-Zurqānī – on the authority of Bilāl ؓ, that when he settled at Dārayyā – the name of a place close to Shām – Bilāl saw the Prophet ﷺ in a dream after his passing, saying, "What is this harshness, O Bilāl? Is the time not ripe for you to visit us?" Thereupon Bilāl awoke full of sadness and fright, so he rode his steed to Medina. When he came to the grave of the Prophet ﷺ, he was brought to tears and began rubbing his face over it. Whereupon al-Ḥasan and al-Ḥusayn ؓ approached, and Bilāl began to hug and kiss them. Then they said to him, "We desire to hear your call to prayer – that which you would make for the Messenger of Allah ﷺ in the mosque." Thus he ascended the roof of the mosque and stood in the place where he used to stand. When he said, "Allah is Great, Allah is Great!" Medina trembled. When he reached the words, "I declare that there is no god besides Allah," its tremor grew. And when he said, "I declare that Muhammad ﷺ is the Messenger of Allah," the women (*ʿawātiq*) left their residences and said, "Has the Messenger of Allah ﷺ been resurrected?" Never was a day witnessed with more men

cried-out, 'What a calamity!' as if she had been taken by force. To this, he ؓ responded, 'O what joy! Tomorrow I shall meet the beloved ones – Muhammad and his Companions.'

---

and women weeping in Medina after him ﷺ than that day." And that was because they were reminded of the Messenger of Allah ﷺ by hearing the call to prayer from his Muezzin ؓ.' Sirāj al-Dīn, ʿAbd-Allāh al-Ḥusaynī, *Sayyidunā muḥammad rasūl-allāh* ﷺ.

Profusely Invoking Blessings and Peace Upon Him ﷺ

Profusely invoking blessings and peace upon him ﷺ is an inseparable manifestation of making much mention of the Messenger of Allah ﷺ, and having true veneration and longing for him. Sufficient for us in establishing the significance of this are the Words of Allah Most High, 'Verily, Allah and His Angels send their blessings upon the Prophet. O you who believe, invoke blessings on him and send your greetings of peace.'[27] Furthermore, he ﷺ said, 'Whoever invokes one blessing upon me, Allah shall send ten [blessings] upon him.' Narrated by Muslim and the authors of the *Sunan*[28].

He ﷺ said, 'Indeed, Jibrīl عليه السلام said to me, "Shall I not give you glad tidings? Indeed, Allah Mighty and Majestic says, 'Whoever invokes blessings upon you, I shall invoke blessings upon him and whoever sends greetings of peace upon you, I shall send greetings of peace upon him'."' Reported by Aḥmad and al-Ḥākim, who also deemed it rigorously authenticated according to his criteria, and as concurred by al-Dhahabī.

27 Qur'an 33:56.

28 Imams al-Tirmidhī, Abū Dāwūd, al-Nasā'ī and Ibn Mājah – each of whom authored hadith collections entitled *al-Sunan*.

Moreover he ﷺ said, 'Indeed, the people who will have the most right to me on the day of resurrection are those who were the most generous in invoking blessings upon me.' Ibn Ḥibbān graded this hadith as rigorously authenticated.

The lovers have the distinction mentioned in the following hadith, on the authority of Anas ibn Mālik ؓ, who stated, 'The Messenger of Allah ﷺ said, "Whoever invokes a blessing upon me, his blessing will reach me and I will invoke a blessing upon him, and ten good deeds are recorded for him besides that.' Narrated by al-Ṭabarānī in *al-Awsaṭ* with a chain of transmission about which there is no objection, and it has a supporting testimony with an authentic chain of narration on the authority of Ibn Masᶜūd ؓ.

Thus invoking blessings upon him ﷺ is equivalent to an intimate discourse with the Prophet ﷺ. You say, 'O Allah, bless our Master Muhammad and grant him peace,' and he ﷺ replies to you, 'May Allah bless you, O So-and-so.'[29] O Allah, make his noble heart ﷺ tender towards us and reward him on our behalf with the best that you have rewarded a prophet on behalf of his nation.

---

29 "ᶜAmmār ibn Yāsir ؓ said to me [ᶜImrān ibn Ḥimyarī], "Should I not relate to you a hadith that the Messenger of Allah ﷺ related to me? 'Verily Allah, Mighty and Majestic, gave one of the angels the ability of hearing all of creation and he will stand over my grave until the final hour rises. Thus there shall not be a single one of my nation who sends a prayer of salutation upon me, except that he will say, "O Aḥmad, So-and-so the son of So-and-so..." by his name and the name of his father, "... has sent prayers upon you in such-and-such a manner." [And the Lord has granted for me] that whoever sends one salutation upon me, He will send ten salutations upon him. And if he were to increase, then so too will Allah Mighty and Majestic'."' Al-Dimashqī, al-Ḥāfiẓ Ibn Nāṣir al-Dīn, *al-Ikhbār fī wafāh al-mukhtār* ﷺ.

PART THREE

The Love of the Prophet ﷺ Demonstrated by the Companions رضي الله عنهم as a Whole

The Companions' Love ﷺ for the Prophet ﷺ

There is no doubt that the love that the Companions had for the Prophet ﷺ was greater than the love for him held by all others, for it was a love borne out of witnessing and observing through their own eyes – and hearing or reading an account is not quite like witnessing with one's own eyes. Even those who entered Islam after initially denying it, did not deny his excellence ﷺ prior to their faith. For they had seen the proofs of his perfection and prophethood. But the tribalism of the era of ignorance and their pride in their forefathers had veiled them from the truth. Then, when the veil was lifted,[30] they believed and their faith and love for him ﷺ grew immensely, to the point that they sacrificed their wealth and lives for him ﷺ.

30 The veil of disbelief that is mentioned in the Qur'an (2:7), 'Allah has set a seal on their hearts and on their hearing, and on their eyes is a veil. Theirs will be an awful doom.' While disbelief itself is considered to be veiling of the truth, 'His Words Most High, "Indeed those that disbelieve," i.e. the polytheists of the Arabs, while al-Kalbī stated, "It refers to the Jews." Linguistically *kufr* (disbelief) is rejection and its linguistic origin is from *al-kufr*, which is a veil. From which the night being referred to as a *kāfir* is derived, for it veils things by its darkness. Farmers are also referred to as *kāfir* for they cover over the seed with soil, and the disbeliever (*kāfir*) covers over the truth with his rejection.' Al-Baghawī, Muḥyī al-Sunnah Abū Muḥammad al-Ḥusayn ibn Masʿūd al-Farrā', *Maʿālim al-tanzīl*.

In this vein, ʿAmr ibn al-ʿĀṣ ؓ said, 'There was no one more beloved to me than the Messenger of Allah ﷺ.'

In a way similar to ʿAmr, was Khālid ibn al-Walīd ؓ, who had initially fought against the Messenger, yet was later guided by his intellect. Thus he entered Islam and expended his life for the sake of Allah and His Messenger ﷺ, to the extent that the Messenger of Allah ﷺ conferred upon him the title of 'the Sword of Allah.' Khālid ibn al-Walīd ؓ said at the time of his own death, 'I took part in a hundred battles and there is not an area of a hand-span upon my body except there is [a mark from] a sword strike or a spear's stab-wound or an arrow shot. Alas, I am dying on my bed just as a camel. May the eyes of the cowards not sleep!'

The reports that illustrate the entirety of the Companions' love for the Prophet ﷺ are many and mass-transmitted. Similarly, the reports of individual Companions' love for him ﷺ are also rigorously authenticated and established. Thus we shall suffice with a summary documentation hereafter.

We begin by reminding ourselves of the states of the Companions for, while they were being tortured with the severest of punishments in Mecca, they would face them with the remembrance of Allah Most High and His Oneness. Bilāl ؓ for instance, would raise his voice saying, 'One, One.'[31] He entwined the bitterness of his torture with the sweetness of faith and love of Allah and His Messenger ﷺ. Thus neither he, nor his fellow Companions, were distressed by the torment despite its severity.

31 Referring to the oneness of Allah and highlighting his rejection of polytheism.

Love During the Battle of Badr[32]

The stories of the participants in the Battle of Badr, who sacrificed their souls out of love for the Messenger of Allah ﷺ – may Allah be pleased with them – are well-known. Regarding the battle's preparation, Saʿd ibn Muʿādh ؓ – among the greatest of the Anṣār[33] – proposed a tent be built to shelter the Prophet ﷺ saying, 'Tribes have not attended [the battle] with you, yet we do not love you more intensely than they. If they had thought you would ever encounter war, they would not have left your side. Allah would have protected you through them, they would have

32 The Battle of Badr took place on 17 Ramadan 2 AH/624 CE at the town of Badr, approximately 150 km south-west of Medina and 50 km inland from the Red Sea. The battle is referred to as, 'the day of criterion,' in the Qur'an (8:41), as all future conquests and victories hinged on the Muslims' victory here. The Messenger of Allah ﷺ set out for battle with 313 men, 2 horses and 70 camels. They encountered a contingent of the Quraysh numbering 1,000, including their leaders, cavalry and brave men. Allah assisted the believers with angels and gave them victory, while 70 disbelievers were slain, including Abū Jahl.

33 Literally meaning 'The Helpers'. They consisted of Muslims from the tribes of ʿAws and Khazraj, who resided in Medina and aided the Prophet ﷺ and his Companions who emigrated from Mecca (Muhājirīn).

been sincere in counsel to you and fought alongside you.' Whereupon the Messenger of Allah ﷺ, praised him well and supplicated for him, asking good for him. Then a tent was built for the Messenger of Allah ﷺ wherein he stayed.

No one stood closer to the Messenger of Allah ﷺ guarding him with the sword on the battlefield of Badr, than Abū Bakr ؓ. When the fight intensified, he ﷺ plunged into the rows of the enemy, wearing a coat of mail and reciting, 'Soon the united front will be routed and will turn and flee.'[34]

This demonstrates the utmost love for the Messenger of Allah ﷺ held by the Companions as a whole. It was a love that comprised of sacrificing the precious and dear, and even the soul – a love in which the Messenger of Allah ﷺ delighted.

34 Qur'an 54:45.

Love During the Battle of al-Rajīʿ[35]

The pagans betrayed a delegation of Qur'anic reciters, killing some of them for resisting capture. Two of the Muslims – Zayd ibn al-Dathinnah and Khubayb ibn ʿAdī ﷺ – surrendered to what was a deceptive promise of the pagans. The pair were taken to Mecca to be killed as vengeance for the blood of some of the pagans killed in the Battle of Badr.

---

35 'In Ṣafar in the third year after the Migration, ʿAḍal and al-Qārah from the tribes of Banū al-Hūn ibn Khuzaymah – relatives of Banū Asad – purported to have Islam within them. They wanted that he ﷺ send those who will teach them about the religion. So he ﷺ sent six men from his Companions along with them: Marthad ibn Abī Marthad al-Ghanawī, Khālid ibn al-Bukayr al-Laythī, ʿĀṣim ibn Thābit ibn Abī al-Aqlaḥ from Banū ʿAmr ibn ʿAwf, Khubayb ibn ʿAdī from Banū Jaḥjabā ibn Kulfah, Zayd ibn al-Dathinnah ibn Bayāḍah ibn ʿAmr and ʿAbd-Allāh ibn Ṭāriq; an ally of Banū Zafar. Marthad was authorised with leading the delegation. They set off with the people until they arrived at al-Rajīʿ – which is the watering place of Hudhayl, close to ʿAsfān. Thereupon ʿAḍal and al-Qārah betrayed them, and called out for help from Hudhayl, who then descended on them with their steeds and threatened them with battle. Thereupon they offered them assurances of safety and said, "We want to claim a ransom for you from the people of Mecca." Marthad, Khālid and ʿĀṣim refused to accept their assurances and fought until they were killed [...] As for the others, they took them captive and left with them to Mecca.' Ibn Khaldūn, Walī al-Dīn ʿAbd al-Raḥmān Muḥammad ibn ʿAbd al-Raḥīm al-Ḥaḍramī al-Ishbīlī, *al-ʿIbr wa dīwān al-mubtadā'*.

The pagans asked Khubayb ﷺ before killing him, 'Would you prefer that Muhammad ﷺ be in your place instead?' He replied, 'No, by Allah, the Immense! I would not want him to ransom me for even a thorn that may prick his foot.'

As for Zayd ibn al-Dathinnah ﷺ, the chief pagan Abū Sufyān said to him, when he was about to kill him, 'I implore you by Allah, O Zayd! In this moment, would you prefer that Muhammad be with us and take your place with his neck being struck, and you be [sat] with your family?' He ﷺ replied, 'By Allah! I would not want that Muhammad ﷺ be where he is right now and be harmed by even a thorn, while I sit among my family!'

Abū Sufyān said, 'I have not seen anyone love another the way that the Companions of Muhammad love Muhammad.' This testament suffices to demonstrate the extent of the love for the Messenger of Allah ﷺ held by all of the Companions, may Allah be pleased with them all.

Love During the Battle of Banū Muṣṭaliq[36]

News reached the Prophet ﷺ that the tribe of Banū Muṣṭaliq, under the leadership of their chief al-Ḥārith ibn Abī Ḍirār, was preparing to wage war against him. So the Prophet ﷺ made a foray against them, whereby a large number of them were taken prisoner, and their womenfolk and children taken captive. A large number of captives were then distributed between the Muslims, and among those taken captive that day was Juwayriyyah, the daughter of al-Ḥārith ibn Abī Ḍirār.

Juwayriyyah agreed to a contract with the one to whom she was allotted, with terms stating that he would grant her freedom in return for a sum

36 'The battle of Banū Muṣṭaliq, the Messenger of Allah ﷺ resided [in Medina] until Shaᶜbān of this, the sixth year. Then he fought Banū al-Muṣṭaliq from Khazāᶜah, when news reached him that they had gathered their forces against him. Their leader was al-Ḥārith ibn Abī Ḍirār, the father of the Mother of the Believers Juwayriyyah. So he set out for them and left Abū Dharr al-Ghifārī ؓ in charge – it has also been said Numaylah ibn ᶜAbd-Allāh al-Laythī was left in charge. He ﷺ met them at al-Muraysīᶜ – one of their watering places lying between Qudayd and the [Red] sea shore. Thereupon they advanced and Allah routed them, with some of them being killed and women and children taken captive; among them was Juwayriyyah ؓ the daughter of their leader al-Ḥārith.' Ibn Khaldūn, Walī al-Dīn ᶜAbd al-Raḥmān Muḥammad ibn ᶜAbd al-Raḥīm al-Ḥaḍramī al-Ishbīlī, *al-ᶜIbr wa dīwān al-mubtadā'*.

of money she would pay him. ʿĀ'ishah ﵂ recalled, 'So she came to the Messenger of Allah ﷺ seeking his assistance in fulfilling this contract. He ﷺ said, "Do you not have a better alternative than that?" She replied, "And what would that be, O Messenger of Allah?" He ﷺ said, "That I fulfil your contract for you and marry you?" She said, "Yes, O Messenger of Allah!" He ﷺ responded, "I have concluded it".'

ʿĀ'ishah ﵂ added, 'The message was sent out to the people that the Messenger of Allah ﷺ had married Juwayriyyah, the daughter of al-Ḥārith ibn Abī Ḍirār. Consequently the people said, "[These are now] in-laws of the Messenger of Allah ﷺ!" Thereupon, they freed whoever was allocated to them – i.e. they freed whatever captives they had, without recompense – for the Countenance of Allah.'

ʿĀ'ishah ﵂ further stated, 'By his marriage to her alone, a hundred households from Banū al-Muṣṭaliq were emancipated. I do not know of a woman who was a greater blessing to her people than her.'

O what love! A hundred households, a hundred families, whose total numbered – as the scholars have mentioned – seven hundred individuals. The monetary value of each one being equivalent to the price of a good car in our times! They were all emancipated only because of the Prophet's marriage ﷺ to a woman from their clan. So simply out of their love for him ﷺ, the Muslims freed the members of her clan without any recompense as they had become in-laws to the Messenger of Allah ﷺ.

Love During the Threat of War at Ḥudaybiyyah

The pagans prevented the Prophet ﷺ and the Muslims from entering Mecca for the ʿUmrah pilgrimage in the year of Ḥudaybiyyah.[37] Thus the Prophet ﷺ proclaimed publicly and repeatedly emphasised – to both the general public and elite – that he had not come to fight but had rather come out of reverence for the House[38], intending to perform the ʿUmrah

---

37 'The Pact of al-Ḥudaybiyyah – it occurred in the month of Dhū al-Qaʿdah at the end of the sixth year following the Migration. Its cause was that the Prophet ﷺ announced he was heading for Mecca to perform the ʿUmrah pilgrimage, thus a large contingent of the Muhājirīn and the Anṣār joined him, approximately 1,400. The Prophet ﷺ entered the state of consecration of *Iḥrām* on the journey and had sent the message ahead guaranteeing the safety of the people from war, so that they may know that he had only set out to visit the House out of veneration for it. While he ﷺ was at Dhū al-Ḥulayfah, he sent a scout from the tribe of Khazāʿah, whose name was Bishr ibn Sufyān, to bring him news about the people of Mecca. He ﷺ travelled on until he reached Ghadīr al-Ashṭāṭ, when the scout arrived and said to him, "Quraysh have gathered forces against you. They have gathered the Abyssinians against you, and they will fight you, block and prevent you from [accessing] the House." [...] Then they [the people of Mecca] sent Suhayl ibn ʿAmr as an envoy on their behalf to draw up a peace treaty between them and the Muslims.' Al-Būṭī, Muḥammad Saʿīd Ramaḍān, *Fiqh al-sīrah al-nabawiyyah*.

38 Referring to the House of Allah; the Kaaba in Mecca.

pilgrimage. Envoys from Quraysh came to discuss the matter, among them was ʿUrwah ibn Masʿūd al-Thaqafī. His hadith is well-known in the collection of al-Bukhārī and others. He narrates that he began to observe the Companions of the Messenger of Allah ﷺ with his own eyes, and said, 'By Allah! The Messenger of Allah ﷺ does not clear his throat, except that his expectoration would fall into the palm of one of them, which he would then rub over his face and body. When he commands them, they rush to carry out his command – i.e. they vie with one another to implement it – and when he performs ablution, they almost fight over [the remnants of] his ablution water. When he speaks, they lower their voices in his presence and they do not look up at him directly out of reverence for him.'

ʿUrwah returned to his companions and said, 'O people, by Allah, I have visited kings as an envoy. I have visited Caesar[39], Chosroes[40] and

39 *Al-Qayṣar*, Caesar, referring to Heraclius (575-641 CE), the Byzantine emperor who in 610 CE inherited a crumbling empire under attack from the Persians and Slavs. He resisted attacks on Constantinople and wrested territories back from the Persians, and later invaded their lands. He made peace with the son of Chosroes II on the condition that the True Cross, which was taken by the Persians should be returned. He himself restored it to the Church of the Holy Sepulchre in 630 CE. The Prophet ﷺ wrote to him and sent Diḥyah al-Kalbī ؓ to him as an emissary to invite him to Islam. By 636 CE, the Muslims had taken the territories of Syria, Egypt and Byzantine Mesopotamia. Heraclius died in 641 CE in Istanbul.

40 *Kisrā*, Chosroes II, the influential Sassanid king of Persia – he reigned between 590 CE and 628 CE. His reign was marked by frequent warring with the Byzantines. ʿAbd-Allāh ibn Hudhāfah al-Sahmī was sent as an envoy with a letter from the Messenger ﷺ to Chosroes, who tore it upon receipt. Upon hearing this, he ﷺ said, 'May Allah obliterate his kingdom!' Kisrā died after a revolt in the royal household upon which he was condemned to death and executed in 628 CE – twelve years prior to the Arab incursion.

al-Najāshī[41]. By Allah, I have never seen a king whose companions revere him as much as the Companions of Muhammad revere Muhammad ﷺ.'

41 Also known as Aṣḥamah, he was an Abyssinian King from 614-631 CE and considered among the Companions who did not migrate to meet the Messenger ﷺ. He gave refuge to a number of the Companions, among them ʿUthmān ibn ʿAffān and Jaʿfar ibn Abī Ṭālib ؓ. ʿAmr ibn Umayyah al-Ḍimrī was sent by the Prophet ﷺ to deliver his letter to al-Najāshī, who placed it over his eyes and descended his throne to read it on the ground, out of respect and humility. Al-Ḥāfiẓ Abū Nuʿaym al-Aṣfahānī narrates in *Ḥilyah al-awliyā'* on the authority of Abū Mūsā al-Ashʿarī ؓ that, 'Al-Najāshī asked Jaʿfar ؓ, "What does your companion say regarding the son of Maryam ؑ?" He replied, "He speaks the Words of Allah Mighty and Majestic, with regards to him: He is the Spirit of Allah and His Word, whom He brought from the virgin maiden that no man had approached and [who] immaculately conceived a child." Whereupon al-Najāshī reached for a twig from the ground, and lifted it up saying, "O assembly of priests and monks! These [people] do not exceed what you say about the son of Maryam, by as much as this [twig]! You are welcome! And the one from whom you have come is welcome! I declare that he is the Messenger of Allah and that he is the one about whom ʿĪsā ؑ gave glad tidings. If it was not for my position in the land, assuredly I would have gone to him, and even kissed his sandal. Reside in my land wherever you please".' He died in Rajab in 9 AH, shortly after the battle of Tabūk, and the Prophet ﷺ prayed his funeral prayer in absentia.

Loving Allah and His Messenger and Acquiring Their Love in Return

❦

Al-Bayhaqī narrates from a Companion among the Anṣār that when the Messenger of Allah ﷺ would perform ablution or clear his throat, they competed over gathering his expectoration and then wiped it over their faces and body. So the Messenger of Allah ﷺ said, 'Why do you do this?' They replied, 'We seek blessing by it.' The Messenger of Allah ﷺ replied, 'Whoever would love for Allah and His Messenger to love him, then let him speak truthfully, discharge his trusts and not harm his neighbour.'

This was his way ﷺ, for their answer encapsulated the meaning of love. Given their great love for his person, to the extent that they wiped themselves with his saliva, he ﷺ guided them to the conduct that would then lead them to Allah and His Messenger's love for them.

Al-Ṭabarānī narrated that 'Abd al-Raḥmān ibn al-Ḥārith al-Sulamī ؓ said, 'We were with the Prophet ﷺ when he called for water. He then immersed his hand in it and performed ablution, so we kept track of it and drank it, whereupon the Prophet ﷺ said, "What prompted you to do what you did?" We said, "Love for Allah and His Messenger." So he replied, "If you would love for Allah and His Messenger to love you, then discharge your trust when you are entrusted, be truthful when you speak and be good neighbours to those who live near to you".'

The Battle of Ḥunayn and The Love of the Anṣār

Al-Bukhārī narrates that Anas ﷺ said, 'When it was the day of Ḥunayn[42], [the tribes of] Hawāzin, Ghaṭafān and others had set out with their livestock and offspring. The Messenger of Allah ﷺ had ten thousand [in his army] and the freed captives [from the Conquest of Mecca],[43] who all

42 The battle took place in 8 AH/630 CE, at the valley of Ḥunayn, located near the city of al-Ṭā'if. 'The Expedition of Ḥunayn occurred when he ﷺ had completed the Conquest of Mecca, and he was informed that Hawāzin had marched to launch an attack against him. So he decided to march to them, with the army of the [Meccan] Conquest and those new Muslims who had joined their ranks. [...] The Muslims initially suffered a defeat. He Most High said, "And on the day of Ḥunayn, when you were impressed with your large numbers but they were of no avail to you..." [9:25]. Al-ʿAbbās ﷺ summoned the people [when the situation was dire], so they came forth. While he ﷺ was sat on his mule, he took a handful of soil and turned towards the disbelievers' faces [and threw the soil]. There was not a single eye in which that soil did not enter. Then Allah Most High revealed (8:17), "And it was not you who threw when you threw, rather it was Allah who threw," Allah then granted them victory.' Al-Mālikī, Sayyid Muḥammad ibn ʿAlawī al-Ḥasanī, *Muhammad the Best of Creation: A Glimpse of his Blessed Life*.

43 'If there was no example of the generosity in his kindness and the preponderance of his forbearance other than what happened on the day of the Conquest of Mecca, then it would have sufficed you regarding him. For he entered it by force and they were abased before him – and they had inflicted the greatest of harm upon him, fooled around with him insolently and had killed his uncles and Companions. Yet he entered it with humility and submission. His beard was on the verge of touching his saddle out

turned their backs on him and fled,[44] until he was left by himself. So he made two distinct proclamations on that day, while he was seated on a white mule. He turned to his right and said, "O congregation of Anṣār!" They replied, "At your service, O Messenger of Allah! Rejoice, we are with you!" Then he turned to his left and said, "O congregation of Anṣār!" They responded, "At your service, O Messenger of Allah! Rejoice, we are with you!" Thereupon, he dismounted and said, "I am the Slave of Allah and His Messenger," and the pagans were resoundingly defeated.'

On that day he ﷺ acquired a vast quantity of the spoils of war, which he shared between the Muhājirīn[45] and the freed captives. He did not give anything to the Anṣār and so some of them said, 'When adversity befalls, we are summoned. Yet the spoils of war are given to other than us?' News of that reached him ﷺ and so he gathered them in a cupola and said, 'O congregation of Anṣār, what news has reached me?' They remained silent. So he said, 'O congregation of Anṣār, are you not pleased that people go [back] with the material world while you go back with the Messenger of Allah, receiving him in your homes?' They said, 'Indeed!' So he ﷺ said, 'If people were to traverse a valley and the Anṣār traversed a mountain trail, I would surely traverse the mountain trail of the Anṣār.'

---

of submission to Allah and humility before Him. He gave a sermon in their midst and said, "What do you think I should do with you?" They replied, "Good! Generous brother and nephew." He replied, "I say just as my brother Yūsuf ﷺ said (12:92), 'No blame will there be upon you today. Allah will forgive you; and He is the Most Merciful of the Merciful.' Go! For you are free." He released them, did right by them and honoured them.' ʿItr, Nūr al-Dīn, *al-Nafaḥāt al-ʿiṭriyyah*.

44 These were members of Quraysh, who had recently embraced Islam following the Conquest of Mecca. They had fled when the Muslims were under fierce attack from the opposition at the commencement of the battle, and the Muslims were forced to retreat.

45 Literally the Migrants, referring to the Companions who had emigrated to Medina from Mecca.

The tribes of Hawāzin and Thaqīf had brought their wealth, livestock, women and children in order to spur their desire to win and ensure they were not defeated. However all of that became the spoils that fell into the hands of the Muslims, to the extent that the houses, tents and dwellings were filled with captives and prisoners of war. The captives and prisoners of war would traditionally become the property of the winning army, yet all of the Anṣār and the Muhājirīn waived their rights over the captives and the prisoners of war, and freed them in order to please the Messenger of Allah ﷺ. And that is the utmost love the Companions had for the Prophet ﷺ.

In relation to that is the following report, 'When the Prophet ﷺ entered Mecca, he stood upon al-Ṣafā[46], beseeching Allah Most High while the Anṣār surrounded him. They said among themselves, "Do you think that when Allah grants the Messenger of Allah ﷺ conquest of his land and city that he will reside therein?" When he finished his supplication, he said, "What did you say?" They replied, "Nothing, O Messenger of Allah." He persisted in asking them until they told him. Thereupon the Messenger of Allah ﷺ said, "I take refuge in Allah! Life is your life, and death is your death".'

Their statement shows their love for him ﷺ and their fear of him leaving them, as well as his love ﷺ for them.[47] In that statement there is also a

46 A mountain in Mecca located near the Kaaba in Mecca. It is mentioned by name in the Qur'an (2:158): 'Behold! Ṣafā and Marwā are among the Symbols of Allah.'

47 '"Indeed, I am the Slave of Allah and His Messenger," i.e. by this description it necessitates that I do not return to a land that I had abandoned for the sake of Allah, and that I do not wish [to reside in] a city from which I migrated unto Allah. Just as Allah has stated (59:9), "Those who entered the city and the faith before them, love those who flee unto them for refuge." Its essence is that the goal of the Migration was to flee unto Allah and that the separation was from the homeland of my people unto your homeland. "Life," i.e. my life, "is your life, and death," i.e. my death, "is your death." The meaning of which is, for as long as I live, I shall live in your lands just as you do,

miracle of the Messenger ﷺ being informed from the unseen, for a soul does not know in which land it shall die.

and when I die, I shall die in your lands just as you; I shall not part from you, neither in life nor in death.' Al-Qārī, al-Mullā ʿAlī ibn Sulṭān Muḥammad, *Mirqāt al-mafātīḥ sharḥ mishkāt al-maṣābīḥ*.

The Companions Vying in the Love of the Messenger of Allah ﷺ

Al-Ṭabarānī narrates that Kaʿb ibn ʿUjrah said, 'We sat one day in a group before the Messenger of Allah ﷺ in the mosque – the congregation of the Anṣār, a group of the Muhājirīn and a group of Banū Hāshim[48]. We were contesting over which one of us was the closest and most beloved to the Messenger of Allah ﷺ.'

'We said, "We, the community of the Anṣār, believed in him, followed him and fought alongside him when his battalion was situated in the middle of his enemy. So we are the closest to the Messenger of Allah and the most beloved to him".'

'While our brothers, the Muhājirīn, said, "We are the ones who migrated with Allah and His Messenger ﷺ, who left kinsfolk, families and wealth behind, and we participated [in the battles] you participated in. We have

---

48 A clan of the tribe of Quraysh, to whom the Messenger ﷺ belonged.

witnessed what you have witnessed. So we are the closest to the Messenger of Allah ﷺ and the most beloved to him".'

'Our brothers from Banū Hāshim said, "We are the kinsfolk of the Messenger of Allah and we participated in what you have participated in. We have witnessed what you have witnessed. So we are the closest to the Messenger of Allah ﷺ and most beloved to him.'

'Whereupon the Messenger of Allah ﷺ came up to us and said, "Did you say something?" So we repeated what we had said, upon which he ﷺ said to the Anṣār, "You spoke the truth! Who can deny this about you?' So we informed him of what our brothers the Muhājirīn had said, to which he replied, "They spoke the truth! Who can deny this about them?" Then we informed him of what our brothers from Banū Hāshim had said, to which he said, "They spoke the truth! Who can deny this about them?"'

'Then he said, "Shall I not judge between you?" We replied, "Indeed, may our fathers and mothers be your ransom, O Messenger of Allah!" He ﷺ said, "As for you, O community of the Anṣār, then I am but your brother," to which they replied, "Allah is the greatest! We have taken him along with us, by the Lord of the Kaaba!" Then he said, "As for you, O Muhājirīn, then I am but from among you," to which they replied, "Allah is the Greatest! We have taken him along with us, by the Lord of the Kaaba!" Then he said, "As for you, O Banū Hāshim, then you are from me and unto me." So we stood up, and each of us was pleased and delighted with the Messenger of Allah ﷺ.'

THE COMPANIONS' FEELINGS OF LOVE FOR THE MESSENGER ﷺ

It is narrated that Anas ibn Mālik ؓ said, 'On the day when the Messenger of Allah ﷺ entered Medina, everything illuminated therein. And when it was the day on which he passed away, everything in Medina fell into darkness.'[49]

Al-Bukhārī narrates, on the authority of Anas ؓ, that, 'A man asked the Prophet ﷺ about the Final Hour, to which he replied, "And what have you prepared for it?" The man responded, "Nothing except that I love Allah and His Messenger ﷺ." He ﷺ said, "You will be with whom you love".' Anas ؓ commented, 'We – the Companions of Muhammad ﷺ – never rejoiced

---

49 '"In the narration of al-Dārimī," i.e. on the authority of Anas ؓ, "Who stated, 'I have never seen a day that was better'," i.e. more splendid to the mind, 'nor more radiant,' i.e. in visible light, 'than the day in which the Messenger of Allah ﷺ came to us,' for that was the day of reunion for those longing for that [moment of] beauty. 'And I did not see a day more unpleasant,' i.e. worse or more saddening to the heart, 'nor darker,' i.e. with the physical eye, 'than the day in which the Messenger of Allah ﷺ passed away.'" For indeed it was the day of separation for the ardent lovers.' Al-Qārī, al-Mullā ʿAlī ibn Sulṭān Muḥammad, *Mirqāt al-mafātīḥ sharḥ mishkāt al-maṣābīḥ*.

at anything as much as we rejoiced at hearing the Prophet's words ﷺ, "You will be with whom you love".' Anas ؓ added, 'For I love the Prophet ﷺ, Abū Bakr and ʿUmar, and I hope to be with them, out of my love for them, even if I did not carry out the like of their actions.'

In another hadith it is narrated, 'A person will be with whomever he loves,' which is similar to the wording at the end of this hadith.

This was the state of all the Companions, as attested to by the following statement of our master ʿAlī ibn Abī Ṭālib, may Allah ennoble his face, 'The Messenger of Allah ﷺ was more beloved to us – i.e. the community of the Companions – than our wealth, children, fathers, mothers and cool water at the point of thirst.' His words, 'more beloved to us,' includes all of the Companions, for it is established that when the Companions would speak with the plural pronoun, as is the case here, what would be intended would be all of the Companions ؓ. May Allah be pleased with them.

PART FOUR

The Love of the Four Rightly Guided Caliphs for the Messenger ﷺ

Abū Bakr the Veracious' Love ﷺ

Al-Bazzār narrates on the authority of our master ʿAlī ibn Abī Ṭālib – while its original chain of transmission is found in the *Ṣaḥīḥ* of al-Bukhārī from the abridged hadith of ʿAbd-Allāh ibn ʿAmr ﷺ – that ʿAlī ﷺ delivered a sermon in which he said, 'O people, who is the bravest man?' They replied, 'You, O Commander of the Faithful!' Whereupon, he said, 'As for me, no one challenged me to a duel except I exacted retribution from him. But the bravest is Abū Bakr ﷺ. We constructed a tent for the Messenger of Allah ﷺ[50] and we said, "Who will remain with the Messenger of Allah ﷺ to ensure none of the pagans pounce on him?" And by Allah, none of us had stepped forward yet, but Abū Bakr ﷺ had already drawn his sword, holding it above the Messenger of Allah's head ﷺ. No one charged at him ﷺ except he would charge towards them. Thus this is the bravest of all men!'

ʿAlī ﷺ also said, 'I saw the Messenger of Allah when he was seized by the Quraysh. One of them confronted him and another was shaking him as

50 [A] On the day of the Battle of Badr.

they said, "Are you the one who has made the gods into one God?" And by Allah, not one of us approached, besides Abū Bakr, who was striking one, fighting with another and shaking another as he said, "Woe unto you! Do you [try to] kill a man who says, "My Lord is Allah!"' Then ʿAlī raised the cloak that he was wearing and cried until his beard became wet. Then he said, 'I implore you by Allah! Who is better – the believer who lived among the people of Firʿawn[51] or Abū Bakr ؓ?' The people fell silent and so ʿAlī said, 'By Allah, surely an hour from [the life] of Abū Bakr is better than the entire time spent on earth by the believer among the people of Firʿawn. That was a man who concealed his faith, while this was a man who professed his faith openly.'

Al-Bayhaqī narrates that Muḥammad ibn Sīrīn said, 'Some men during ʿUmar's ؓ era spoke as though they preferred ʿUmar ؓ over Abū Bakr ؓ. When news of that reached ʿUmar ؓ, he said, "By Allah, truly one of Abu Bakr's ؓ nights is better than the family of ʿUmar, and certainly one of Abū Bakr's days is better than the family of ʿUmar!"'

On the night he departed for the cave, the Messenger of Allah ﷺ had left together with Abū Bakr ؓ. Sometimes Abu Bakr would walk in front of him and sometimes he walked behind him ﷺ until the Messenger of

51 Referring to the individual mentioned in the Qur'an (40:28): 'And a believing man of Pharaoh's family, who hid his faith, said: Would you kill a man because he says, "My Lord is Allah" and has brought you clear proofs from your Lord? If he is lying, then his lie is upon him and if he is truthful, then some of what he warns you will befall you. Truly Allah guides not one who transgresses and lies.' 'The scholars have differed over this believer. Muqātil and al-Suddī have stated that he was a Coptic man – the son of the paternal uncle of Pharaoh and he is the one whom Allah spoke of when he said (28:20), "And a man came from the farthest end of the city, running." A group of scholars have also stated that he was an Israelite.' Al-Baghawī, Muḥyī al-Sunnah Abū Muḥammad al-Ḥusayn ibn Masʿūd al-Farrā', *Maʿālim al-tanzīl*.

Allah ﷺ noticed and said, "O Abū Bakr, why do you walk behind me for some time and then in front of me for some time?" He replied, "I remember the bounty hunt, so I walk behind you. Then I remember the ambush, so I walk in front of you".'

'So he said, "O Abū Bakr, if anything would befall me, would you prefer it to befall you instead of me?" He replied, "Yes, by the One who sent you." As they reached the cave, Abū Bakr said, "Stay as you are until I check the cave is all clear." He entered and checked that it was all clear. When he remembered that he had not checked a hole, he said, "Stay as you are until I check all is clear." Then he entered and checked that it was all clear once more. Then he said, "Alight, O Messenger of Allah!" Thereupon he ﷺ alighted.' Then ʿUmar ؓ said, 'By the One in whose hand is my soul, that night was surely better than the family of ʿUmar.'

Before Islam, Abū Bakr ؓ was known among his kinsfolk for tracking down the missing, maintaining family ties, carrying the burden of the weary, being hospitable to guests, donating charity to the poor and assisting those afflicted by vicissitudes decreed by the Real. He was known not to indulge in sin in the pre-Islamic era, being soft-hearted and compassionate with the weak – and these are all among the traits of the Prophet ﷺ. So it is of no surprise that he was drawn to him ﷺ and was the first man to believe in his religion.

Abū Bakr ؓ had the greatest influence in propagating Islam. He was a merchant who was well-acquainted with the people and would propagate Islam and call people to the Messenger of Allah ﷺ. Thus many accepted Islam at his hand such as Saʿd ibn Abī Waqqāṣ ؓ, ʿAbd al-Raḥmān ibn ʿAwf ؓ, ʿUthmān ibn ʿAffān ؓ, Ṭalḥah ؓ, al-Zubayr ؓ, Saʿīd ibn Zayd ؓ and others, may Allah be pleased with them all.

He spent from his wealth for the pleasure of the Messenger ﷺ and in service of his religion. He freed a great number of slaves, among them Bilāl ibn Abī Rabāḥ, ʿĀmir ibn Fuhayrah, Umm ʿUbays, Zinnīrah, al-Nahdiyyah and her daughter, and the freed slave-girl of Banū Muʾammil and others ؓ. He was so prodigious in this regard that he was given the epithet 'the Patron of Freedom' and 'the Emancipator of Slaves'.

That is how he expended his wealth in service of the Messenger of Allah ﷺ. Furthermore he took all his wealth with him during the migration to Medina. Then whenever the occasion arose to spend for a needy cause, he would be the first to give from his wealth. How many times did he spend all of his wealth for the sake of the Messenger of Allah ﷺ, not leaving anything behind for his family besides Allah and His Messenger ﷺ! All of that was in seeking the Countenance of Allah. The following noble verses were revealed in regards to him ؓ: 'And far removed from it (the fire) will be the most God-fearing: he who gives his wealth to purify [himself], and not for [the sake of] one who has with him a favour to be rewarded in return, but only the desire to seek the Countenance of his Lord Most High. Verily, soon he shall be pleased.'[52]

Regarding Saʿd ibn Abī Waqqāṣ' embrace of Islam at his hand ؓ, Quranic verses from the chapter of Luqmān ؓ were revealed, among them: 'And follow the way of the one who has turned [in repentance] unto Me.'[53]

Abū Bakr ؓ was the most beloved of the Companions to the Messenger of Allah ﷺ. ʿUmar ؓ said, 'Abū Bakr is our master, the best of us and the most beloved of us to the Messenger of Allah ﷺ.' Abu Bakr ؓ was also the greatest of the Companions in terms of their love for the Messenger ﷺ.

---

52 Qurʾan 92:17-21.
53 Qurʾan 31:15.

In addition, he was the most knowledgeable regarding the Messenger of Allah ﷺ. According to a famous[54] rigorously-authenticated hadith from the Prophet's sermon ﷺ towards the end of his life, the Messenger ﷺ said, 'Indeed, a slave was given the choice by Allah between having whatever he wishes of the splendour of the world or what He has [in store for him]. So he chose what He has [in store for him].' Thereupon Abū Bakr said, 'May our fathers and mothers be ransomed for you, O Messenger of Allah ﷺ!' The hadith narrator stated, 'So we were surprised. The Messenger was the one given the choice and Abū Bakr was the most knowledgeable regarding him among us.'

The Prophet ﷺ then said, 'There is no man who has benefitted us greater through his company and what his hand possesses than Ibn Abī Quḥāfah[55]. And if I were to select a close friend, I surely would have selected Ibn Abī Quḥāfah.' Another narration has the wording, 'Abū Bakr.'[56]

In another hadith from the sermon, the Messenger of Allah ﷺ said, 'No one has favoured us except we have reciprocated it – with the exception of Abū Bakr, who has favoured us, for which Allah will recompense him on the day of resurrection. And never has the wealth of anyone benefitted me as much as the wealth of Abū Bakr.'

At the end of the sermon, the Prophet ﷺ said, 'No door shall remain [constantly open] in the mosque except for the door of Abū Bakr.' In a

---

54 *Mashhūr*.

55 One of the names of Abū Bakr ؓ.

56 'Then the Messenger of Allah ﷺ said, "Truly, the one with the greatest favour over me, among people through his companionship and his wealth, is Abū Bakr. And if I were to take a dear friend (*khalīl*) besides my Lord, truly I would have taken Abū Bakr".' Narrated by al-Bukhārī in his *Ṣaḥīḥ*.

variant narration, he ﷺ added, 'except what [remains] of the door of Abū Bakr, for I have seen a light over it.'

This latter narration is an indication of his reign as caliph, i.e. that his door alone will remain [open], which was a small door from his house that opened directly into the mosque. His door was to remain open due to his need to look into the affairs of the Muslims. The hadiths referring to the legitimacy of his caliphate are many. While the Companions and the Household of the Messenger of Allah ﷺ also concurred upon the legitimacy of his caliphate, may Allah be pleased with them all.[57]

---

[57] ʿAbū Hurayrah ؓ said thrice, "By Allah, the one who besides there is no god but He, if it was not for Abū Bakr becoming caliph, Allah would not have been worshipped." Abū Hurayrah ؓ spoke the truth, for when the Messenger of Allah ﷺ died, it dazed the Companions and stunned their intellects, and the Bedouin-Arabs apostasised and hypocrisy grew. While he ؓ was the one who remained steadfast at that time, when the greatest of tribulations split the hearts and caused mountains to collapse. During his caliphate he also set out to fight the Bedoun-Arabs, so ʿAlī – may Allah ennoble his face – said, "Where to, O caliph of the Messenger of Allah? I say to you that which the Messenger of Allah ﷺ said to you on the day of Uḥud: Be on the lookout for your sword, do not afflict us with distress through yourself, and return to Medina. For, by Allah, truly if we were afflicted with [the loss of] you, Islam will never have genuine authority". Al-Maqdisī, al-ʿAllāmah Marʿī ibn Yūsuf al-Karamī al-Ḥanbalī, *Talkhīṣ awṣāf al-muṣṭafā* ﷺ *wa dhikr man baʿdahu min al-khulafā*.

ʿUMAR IBN AL-KHAṬṬĀB'S LOVE ﷺ

Prior to embracing Islam, ʿUmar ؓ was staunchly set against the Muslims, while his embrace of Islam would prove to be of immense support to the religion. He ؓ was the answer to the prayer of the Messenger of Allah ﷺ, 'O Allah, strengthen Islam with the most beloved of the two ʿUmars to you: ʿAmr ibn Hishām (Abū Jahl) or ʿUmar ibn al-Khaṭṭāb.' With ʿUmar's embrace of Islam, the Muslims felt empowered and the Prophet ﷺ brought the Companions out into the open and circumambulated the House [of Allah], without them being fearful of anyone.[58]

He spent his life and everything precious in sacrifice for the Prophet ﷺ, and he embodied the sentiment of the Messenger of Allah ﷺ being

---

[58] 'He accepted Islam in the sixth year of prophethood, when he was twenty-seven years old. His Islam came after the acceptance of Islam by forty men. When he accepted Islam, the pagans said, "The people have split from us." And Allah revealed (8:64), "O Prophet! Allah is Sufficient for you and those who follow you among the believers." And Jibrīl ؑ descended and said, "O Muhammad! The celestial residents have given you the glad tidings of the Islam of ʿUmar ؓ." He – upon him be peace and blessings – said, "O Allah! Strengthen Islam through ʿUmar ibn al-Khaṭṭāb".' Al-Maqdisī, al-ʿAllāmah Marʿī ibn Yūsuf al-Karamī al-Ḥanbalī, *Talkhīṣ awṣāf al-muṣṭafā* ﷺ *wa dhikr man baʿdahu min al-khulafā*.

more beloved to him than his own self, as narrated in the aforementioned hadith of al-Bukhārī.

The intensity of his love reached such a degree that a number of his statements conformed with subsequent revelation[59]. ʿAbd-Allāh ibn ʿUmar ؓ narrates that the Messenger of Allah ﷺ said, 'Indeed, Allah has placed the truth upon the tongue of ʿUmar and his heart.' Ibn ʿUmar ؓ also stated, 'Never did a matter befall the people wherein they expressed their opinion regarding it and ʿUmar too expressed his opinion – or Ibn al-Khaṭṭāb spoke regarding it – except that the Qurʾan would be revealed, in accordance with ʿUmar's opinion.'

An example of his love is illustrated in the established narration where he ؓ stated, 'I sought permission from the Prophet ﷺ to perform the ʿUmrah pilgrimage and he gave me consent and said, "Do not forget me in your prayers, my dear younger brother".' ʿUmar ؓ stated, 'They were words that I would not be happy to exchange for the world.' Referring to the words, 'O my dear younger brother,' that were spoken to him.

It is narrated in a rigorously-authenticated hadith that ʿUmar ibn al-Khaṭṭāb ؓ said, 'I entered upon the Messenger of Allah ﷺ while he was [lying] upon a mat. So I sat down and he ﷺ was only wearing his sarong and [I noticed] the mat had marked his side. I also noticed a small pile[60] of barley, four kilograms or so[61], Sanṭ tree pods in one of the corners of the room and a hanging animal-skin. Thereupon my eyes began to well up with tears. So he asked, "What makes you cry, O Ibn al-Khaṭṭāb?" I replied, "O Prophet of Allah, how can I not cry when this mat has marked your side and I do not see anything in your possession except what I see

---

59 *Muwāfaqāt li al-waḥy.*
60 *Qabḍah*, literally a handful.
61 One *Ṣāʿ*, a measure of weight equivalent to approximately four kilograms.

before me. While Chosroes and Caesar enjoy the fruits and rivers, yet you are the Prophet of Allah and His Chosen One and these are all your possessions!' He ﷺ replied, "O Ibn al-Khaṭṭāb, are you not pleased that we will have the Afterlife while they have this world?"' In another rigorously-authenticated hadith, it states, 'They are a people for whom their delights have been paid in advance in their worldly life.'

Stemming from his love for the Prophet ﷺ was his intense love for the Household of the Prophet ﷺ, as was the trait of all the Companions. For that reason, ʿUmar would give them gifts abundantly and prioritise them over others, and al-Ḥasan and al-Ḥusayn were particularly dear to him.

Above all else he would hold our master ʿAlī ibn Abī Ṭālib dear and he would not decide on important matters until he had consulted him. Regarding this, two of his wise sayings became widespread, 'Can there be a judgement without the father of al-Ḥasan?' and 'If it was not for ʿAlī, surely ʿUmar would have perished.' Our master ʿAlī would advise him with the utmost concern and sincerity. When ʿUmar travelled to Jerusalem, he appointed Ali to take charge of all matters related to the governance of Medina.

So do not pay any attention to whoever fabricates history and alters the biography of ʿUmar or any of the other rightly-guided caliphs[62] from

---

62 The Prophet ﷺ stated in a hadith reported by al-Tirmidhī, on the authority of al-ʿIrbād ibn al-Sāriyah, 'I admonish you to have the fear of Allah, listen and obey, even if a slave were to assume leadership over you. For whoever among you shall live will see much discord. Thus my way and the way of the righty-guided caliphs behoves you – hold onto it with your molars.' "'And the way of the rightly-guided caliphs," i.e. those steeped in guidance and, by consensus, they are the four: Abū Bakr, ʿUmar, ʿUthmān and ʿAlī, may Allah be pleased with them all.' Al-ʿĪd, Ibn Daqīq Muḥammad ibn ʿAlī al-Qushayrī, *Sharḥ al-arbaʿīn al-nawawiyyah*.

their sheer purity. Know that the Muslims until the end of the reign of ʿAlī ☺ were a single united group – none of the Muslims harboured any issue in their mind regarding the matter of the caliphate or who was most entitled to it.

Regarding the special brotherhood and the distinct mutual love between ʿAlī ☺ and ʿUmar ☺, we make mention that our master ʿAlī ☺ gave away his daughter Umm Kulthūm ☺ – who was his daughter from Lady Fāṭimah al-Zahrāʾ ☺ in marriage to our master ʿUmar ☺. He also named three of his sons ʿUmar, Abū Bakr and ʿUthmān respectively. A person does not name his sons except with the names most beloved to him and after those he views as great exemplars.

In a reliably established hadith of ʿĀʾishah ☺, the Messenger of Allah ☺ said, 'From time to time, among the nations [of prophets], there are preternatural speakers[63] – i.e. those inspired, as mentioned in a separate narration – and if there was one in my nation, then it is ʿUmar ibn al-Khaṭṭāb.'[64]

---

63 *Muḥaddathūn*, literally those who have been spoken to. '"*Muḥaddathūn*," i.e divinely inspired people just as Ibn Wahb has explained. "Thus if there was one in my nation," i.e. one of them for whom it was assigned and decreed, "then it is ʿUmar ibn al-Khaṭṭāb," i.e. if there were to be more, then he would be the most deserving and most apparent [of them]. Al-Tūribishtī stated, "In their terminology, the *Muḥaddath* is a man whose intuitive judgement proves to be true and accurate. And he in reality is one whose heart is inspired by something of the Celestial Gathering [of angels], and so it is as though He has spoken with him".' Al-Qārī, al-Mullā ʿAlī ibn Sulṭān Muḥammad, *Mirqāt al-mafātīḥ sharḥ mishkāt al-maṣābīḥ*.
64 'The Prophet ☺ said regarding him ☺: "If there were a prophet after me, it truly would have been ʿUmar." He ☺ said, "Indeed Allah placed the truth upon the tongue of ʿUmar and his heart, and he is al-Fārūq – Allah differentiated between the truth and falsehood through him." And he ☺ said, "Indeed ʿUmar is the lamp of the people of paradise." And he ☺ said, "There is not an angel in heaven except that he venerates ʿUmar and there is

It has been widely narrated by a group of the Companions that the Prophet ﷺ said, 'I saw a palace of gold in Paradise, so I asked, "Whose is it?" The reply came back, "It belongs to ʿUmar ibn al-Khaṭṭāb".' May Allah be pleased with him and may He make him pleased.

---

not a devil upon earth except that he distances himself from ʿUmar." [...] And he ﷺ said, "ʿUmar is with me and I am with ʿUmar, and after me the truth is with ʿUmar, wherever he be".' Al-Maqdisī, al-ʿAllāmah Marʿī ibn Yūsuf al-Karamī al-Ḥanbalī, *Talkhīṣ awṣāf al-musṭafā* ﷺ *wa dhikr man baʿdahu min al-khulafā.*

ʿUthmān ibn ʿAffān's Love ﷺ

Our master ʿUthmān ibn ʿAffān was among the very first people to accept Islam. He had a lofty rank and endured great suffering for the sake of Allah, while he constantly grew in love for the Prophet ﷺ and he ﷺ grew in love for him too. His life thrived with the most momentous feats.[65]

When the two sons of Abū Lahab[66] annulled their marriages to the daughters of the Messenger of Allah, Ruqayyah and Umm Kulthūm, at

65 'He assumed leadership of the caliphate and undertook the task after ʿUmar ﷺ in the most consummate manner. He had a wonderful life, demonstrated justice and was scrupulous, abstinent, forbearing, with deep bashful humility and was exceptionally modest. A young servant-boy would take a seat behind him [on his steed] during his caliphate and he would not take exception to that. He would feed the people the food of the royals and enter his house and eat [bread with] vinegar and olive oil. He would give sermon to the people in a sarong, the cost of which, was four or five dirhams. He would fast the day and stand the night in prayer, completing the entire Qur'an in a single unit of prayer. His praiseworthy qualities are more than what can be enumerated.' Al-Maqdisī, al-ʿAllāmah Marʿī ibn Yūsuf al-Karamī al-Ḥanbalī, *Talkhīṣ awṣāf al-musṭafā ﷺ wa dhikr man baʿdahu min al-khulafā.*

66 Literally meaning 'father of flames,' a reference to his ruddy complexion. He is mentioned in the Qur'an (111:1): 'Perish the hands of Abū Lahab! Perish he, too!' He was ʿAbd al-ʿUzzā ibn ʿAbd al-Muṭṭalib, a paternal uncle of the Prophet ﷺ, a pagan and staunch opponent of the Prophet ﷺ and Islam.

the behest of their father and out of spite for the Messenger of Allah, ʿUthmān immediately proposed to Ruqayyah ﵂. The Messenger of Allah ﷺ gave her in marriage to him. Whenever ʿUthmān ﵁ would thank her for something, in return she ﵂ would show appreciation for his company, which had given her much joy.

Our master ʿUthmān ﵁ endured much torment from the pagans and twice migrated with his wife to Abyssinia. When Ruqayyah ﵂ passed away, the love between him and the Messenger of Allah ﷺ had reached such a point that the Prophet ﷺ married his second daughter, Umm Kulthūm ﵂ to him in the third year after the Migration.

The Prophet ﷺ stated in a hadith, 'O ʿUthmān, this is Jibrīl, he has informed me that Allah has married Umm Kulthūm to you in accordance with the like of Ruqayyah's bridal dowry and the like of her companionship.'

If it was not for the utmost love of the Messenger ﷺ for ʿUthmān ﵁, and ʿUthmān's utmost love for the Messenger of Allah ﷺ, he would not have given his second daughter in marriage to ʿUthmān ﵁. It indicates his absolute trust in ʿUthmān ﵁ for the future and it is indeed a great virtue, for it is not known among any of the previous nations that a man had ever married two daughters of a prophet besides ʿUthmān ibn ʿAffān ﵁.[67]

---

67 'The Prophet ﷺ married his two daughters, Ruqayyah and Umm Kulthūm, to him and no one has ever been known to have married two daughters of a prophet besides him. For that reason he was named 'The holder of two lights' (*Dhū al-Nūrayn*). The Prophet ﷺ said about him, "If I had forty daughters, truly I would have married them to him one by one until none would remain, and I did not marry my two daughters to him except through revelation from Allah".' Al-Maqdisī, al-ʿAllāmah Marʿī ibn Yūsuf al-Karamī al-Ḥanbalī, *Talkhīṣ awṣāf al-musṭafā* ﷺ *wa dhikr man baʿdahu min al-khulafā*.

Our master ʿUthmān ؓ was modest and noble, to the extent that the angels were shy of him, as has been established in hadith. He did his utmost to please Allah and His Messenger ﷺ and was famed for having equipped the army of al-ʿUsrah[68] for the Battle of Tabūk[69]. During the time of al-ʿUsrah, when there was a scarcity of wealth among the people, ʿUthmān ؓ undertook the responsibility of equipping the army, to the extent that he did not leave the army in need of a camel's halter nor its reins.

Our master ʿUthmān ؓ conferred nine hundred and forty camels and sixty horses on the army of al-ʿUsrah. While in another narration it states, 'Three hundred camels together with their saddles and saddle-blankets in the path of Allah.' This latter figure may have been the initial donation, which was then later added to, to make up the aforementioned total – may Allah be pleased with him. This caused the Prophet ﷺ to say, 'Whatever ʿUthmān does after today will not harm him,' which he repeated numerous times. ʿUthmān ؓ also made a further donation of a thousand golden dinars[70], which he poured into the lap of the Messenger of Allah ﷺ. Thus it is of no surprise that the Messenger of Allah ﷺ said this to him.

68 i.e. the army of the time of hardship.

69 'Its cause, which Ibn Saʿd and others have narrated, is that news reached the Muslims from the Nabateans – who would go between Syria and Medina for trade – that the Byzantines had gathered forces and that their vanguards had reached the region of al-Balqā'. They had conscripted to their ranks the tribes of Lakhm and Judhām and others among the Christian-Arabs, that were under their command. Whereupon the Prophet ﷺ assigned people to set out. Al-Ṭabarānī relates from the hadith of Ibn Ḥuṣayn that, "The army of the Byzantines was 40,000 soldiers strong." This occurred in the month of Rajab in the year 9 AH. [...] When they eventually reached Tabūk, they did not encounter any ruse nor any fighting, for they had disappeared from sight and those that had gathered to fight had dispersed. [...] He ﷺ arrived back in Medina in Ramadan in the same year and he had been absent for approximately two months.' Al-Būṭī, Muḥammad Saʿīd Ramaḍān, *Fiqh al-sīrah al-nabawiyyah.*

70 [A] One dinar is equivalent to five grams of gold.

In order to realise the value of this expenditure, I will tell you that a camel is equivalent to ten sheep that are suitable for sacrificial offering, and that a single dinar is at least equivalent to a single sacrificial animal or possibly even two. So the words of the Messenger of Allah ﷺ regarding him oblige you to cast aside the spurious allegations of he who has no knowledge of ʿUthmān and his authority as caliph, for his authority was established from the era of the Prophet ﷺ, Abū Bakr ؓ and ʿUmar ؓ.

His status reached such an elevated level with the Prophet ﷺ, that he sent Uthman ؓ as his representative to the Quraysh in the year of the expedition of al-Ḥudaybiyyah. When he was delayed in returning, the Muslims thought that the Quraysh had killed him. Consequently, the Prophet ﷺ summoned the people to the Pledge of al-Riḍwān to fight the pagans in order to avenge the shedding of ʿUthmān's blood. Thereupon, the Companions swore their pledge to him beneath a tree and the Prophet ﷺ took one of his own noble hands and said, 'This is on behalf of ʿUthmān,' and he pledged with it by placing it above his other hand. It was a virtue that was afforded exclusively for ʿUthmān – the Messenger of Allah's hand ﷺ was better for him, than what any of their hands were for themselves, may Allah be pleased with them all.

ʿUthmanʾs life flourished with the most momentous of acts: he adhered closely to the Prophet ﷺ from the moment he returned to Medina after migrating to Abyssinia, and he contributed with everything that was possible for him. His caliphate later attained great success with tremendous conquests.

An example that clearly illustrates his virtue and utmost love for the Messenger of Allah ﷺ is found in the following dialogue, in which he debated with the Khawārij[71] when they besieged him in his home. It is recorded in a narration, whose chain of transmission has been confirmed by the scholars of hadith in accordance with their meticulous conditions. On the authority of Thumāmah ibn Ḥazn al-Qushayrī, a Successor[72] and a renowned and reliable hadith narrator who lived during the Prophet's era ﷺ without having met him ﷺ – may Allah Most High have mercy on him – stated:

> I was present at the home of ʿUthmān ؓ when he looked out over them and said, 'Will you bring your two companions that have incited you against me?' So they were brought [before him] just as two camels or donkeys would have been brought. ʿUthmān looked out over them and said, 'I implore you by Allah and Islam! Do you know that when the Messenger of Allah ﷺ arrived in Medina and there was no water therein to quench thirst besides the well of Rūmah, he ﷺ said, "Who will purchase the well of Rūmah and place its drawing-bucket among those of the Muslims, in exchange for what is better than it in paradise?" So I purchased it with my own wealth, and today you prevent me from drinking from it, such that I must drink sea-water!' They replied, 'By Allah, yes!'
>
> ʿUthmān ؓ said, 'I implore you by Allah and Islam! Do you know that when the mosque could not accommodate its people, and the Messenger of Allah ﷺ said, "Who will purchase the plot of

71 An extreme sect characterised by misplaced religious zeal, who consider those who commit major sins to be disbelievers. 'Al-Khawārij, all of their various denominations agree upon the Slave [of Allah] becoming a disbeliever through sin and they deem ʿUthmān, ʿAlī, Ṭalḥah, al-Zubayr and ʿĀ'ishah ؓ to be disbelievers.' Al-Rāzī, Fakhr al-Dīn, *Iʿtiqādāt firaq al-muslimīn wa al-mushrikīn.*

72 *Tābiʿī*, one who accompanied the Companions but did not meet the Messenger ﷺ.

land of the family of so-and-so in order to extend the mosque in exchange for what is better than it in paradise?" So I purchased it with my own wealth, and today you prevent me from praying two units of prayer therein!' They replied, 'By Allah, yes!'

Then he said, 'I implore you by Allah and Islam! Do you know that it was I who equipped the army of al-ʿUsrah with my wealth?' They replied, 'By Allah, yes!'

He then said, 'I implore you by Allah and Islam! Do you know that the Messenger of Allah ﷺ was upon [Mount] Thabīr of Mecca, and Abū Bakr, ʿUmar and myself were with him when the mountain shook. So much so, that its rocks began to fall to the foot of the mountain. Whereupon he stamped it with his foot and said, "Be still, O Thabīr, for upon you is a Prophet, a truly veracious individual[73] and two martyrs?"' They replied, 'By Allah, yes!' Then ʿUthmān said thrice, 'Allah is the greatest! They have testified for me, by the Lord of the Kaaba, that I am a martyr.'

All of these aforementioned points are established through many rigorously-authenticated hadiths, in addition to his many other great merits and praiseworthy character traits. May Allah be pleased with him.

A number of rigorously-authenticated hadiths from a group of the Companions mention the Prophet ﷺ foretelling the tribulation in which our master ʿUthmān would be killed unjustly, while he remained steadfast upon the truth. Among them is the hadith of ʿAbd-Allāh ibn ʿUmar in which he said, 'The Messenger of Allah ﷺ mentioned a tribulation as a

---

73 *Siddīq*, the epithet of Abū Bakr.

man happened to pass by. Whereupon he ﷺ said, "This masked individual will be killed during it. On that day, he will be treated unjustly".' ʿAbd-Allāh ibn ʿUmar ؓ said, 'So I looked and, lo and behold, it was ʿUthmān ibn ʿAffān ؓ.'

From his modesty and concern for the people, ʿUthmān prohibited the Companions, guards and slaves from fighting to defend him. He ؓ said, 'May a cupping glass of blood – which is the size of a small glass – not be spilt for my sake.' He took an oath that they return and he said to his slaves, 'Whoever among you throws down his weapons is free.' There was a great group of seven hundred in his home, and had he allowed them to fight for him they certainly would have fought the Khawārij until they had driven them away.

ʿUthmān spoke about his murder on his final day, saying, 'Surely, a group of people will kill me.' Then he ؓ said, 'I saw the Prophet ﷺ in a dream, and with him were Abū Bakr ؓ and ʿUmar ؓ. The Prophet ﷺ said, "O ʿUthmān, break fast with us [tomorrow]".'[74] So he awoke fasting on the day that he was killed. May Allah be pleased with him and may He cause him to be pleased, reward him abundantly for his service to the Qur'an and to Islam, and may He elevate his final resting place.

---

[74] 'The Prophet ﷺ informed of his murder and said, "'Uthmān will be killed while he is reciting from the copy of the Qur'an and his blood will flow over His Words Most High (2:137), 'And Allah will suffice you against them'." So it was as he ﷺ had said, and ʿUthmān was martyred in his home with the copy of the Qur'an in front of him and his blood splashed over this verse, "And Allah will suffice you against them, and He is the All-Hearing, the All-Knowing," just as it was said, and that is well known about him. That occurred on Friday the 8th of Dhū al-Ḥijjah, and it has also been said to have occurred during the middle of the days of *tashrīq*. Al-Zubayr prayed [the funeral prayer] over him and he was buried in the Baqīʿ cemetery. His caliphate lasted twelve days short of twelve years, and he was 82 years of age.' Al-Maqdisī, al-ʿAllāmah Marʿī ibn Yūsuf al-Karamī al-Ḥanbalī, *Talkhīṣ awṣāf al-muṣṭafā* ﷺ *wa dhikr man baʿdahu min al-khulafā*.

ʿAlī ibn Abī Ṭālib's Love ﷺ

ʿAlī ibn Abī Ṭālib was the paternal cousin of the Messenger of Allah ﷺ and his foster-son. He was born approximately five years before the start of the Prophetic mission, while it has also been said 'ten years prior.' When financial hardship struck the people of Mecca, Abū Ṭālib – ʿAlī's father – had many dependents. The Prophet ﷺ made an agreement with his uncle al-ʿAbbās ؓ to lighten Abū Ṭālib's burden, with each of them fostering one of his sons. Thus the Prophet ﷺ agreed to foster ʿAlī and al-ʿAbbās agreed to foster Jaʿfar ibn Abī Ṭālib ؓ.

When the Prophet ﷺ had begun receiving revelation, ʿAlī ؓ had entered upon him ﷺ one day while he was praying with his wife Khadījah ؓ, so he asked them about the religion. He ﷺ told him about that which Allah had sent him for, and invited him to Islam. ʿAlī went away and returned the next day and embraced Islam with the Messenger ﷺ. He began to pray alongside him ﷺ, both at home and in the mountain trails. ʿAlī ؓ was a guide, bringing people to the Prophet ﷺ.

When the Prophet ﷺ migrated, he tasked ʿAlī with sleeping in his place to mislead the pagans – and so he did, not caring about the danger. Then after the Prophet's successful departure, he delivered the trusts left by the Messenger ﷺ to their rightful owners. This task of his was a completion of Abū Bakr's ؓ duty in accompanying the Prophet ﷺ, and a sign of his willingness to undertake immense risk and face great danger.

Following the Migration, the Prophet ﷺ paired ʿAlī ؓ and Sahl ibn Ḥunayf ؓ as brothers, according to the preferred view of a number of the Prophet's biographers ؒ. Al-Tirmidhī ؒ narrates a tradition, which he graded as authentic[75], whereby the Prophet ﷺ paired himself with ʿAlī ؓ as brothers.

While ʿAlī ؓ was residing in Medina, he exerted himself in those affairs that the Prophet ﷺ loved. For instance, he once knew that the Prophet ﷺ had a particular need. So he went to the land of a Jewish man and drew water for the owner to farm with. He did so until he had collected seventeen dates for the Prophet ﷺ in exchange for having drawn seventeen buckets of water. So the Prophet ﷺ said, 'Did you undertake this out of love of Allah and His Messenger?' He replied, 'Yes, O Prophet of Allah.'

In the second year after the Migration, he married Fāṭimah ؓ, the Prophet's daughter, and he lived a life of asceticism with her – a life that the Prophet ﷺ had chosen for himself and the people of his household. He ﷺ also nicknamed him 'Abū Turāb'[76] out of love and affection.

---

75 *Ḥasan.*

76 Meaning, 'The holder of soil,' a nickname derived from an incident when ʿAlī's side ؓ was covered in dust and soil (*turāb*). Al-Bukhāri narrates, on the authority of Sahl ibn Saʿd al-Sāʿidī ؓ, that he said, 'No name was more beloved to ʿAlī than Abū Turāb and he would truly delight if he were called by it. The Messenger of Allah ﷺ came to the house of Fāṭimah ؓ and he did not find ʿAlī in the house, so he asked, "Where is your uncle's son?" She replied, "Something occurred between me and him and he became upset with me, and so he left without taking a siesta besides me." Thereupon the

Moreover, ʿAlī held the status of being beloved to the Messenger of Allah ﷺ. During the Battle of Khaybar[77], the Muslims found one of the fortresses difficult to penetrate. So the Messenger of Allah ﷺ said, 'Truly tomorrow I will give the banner to a man who loves Allah and His Messenger, and Allah and His Messenger love him.' Upon hearing that, the senior Companions waited in anticipation for it, each hoping that he would be bestowed with that honour. Then the Messenger ﷺ called ʿAlī ؓ – who had been suffering from an eye ailment – and so he came forth. The Messenger ﷺ sprinkled some of his saliva on to his eyes and supplicated for ʿAlī. He recovered, such that it was as though he had never suffered any ailment at all. Then he ﷺ gave him the banner and Allah gave triumph at his hands.[78]

Messenger of Allah ﷺ said to an individual, "Look for where he is." So the man returned and said, "O Messenger of Allah, he is sleeping in the mosque." So the Messenger of Allah ﷺ came while he was lying down, and ʿAlī's sarong had slipped from his side and some soil had gotten stuck to him. So the Messenger of Allah ﷺ began wiping it from him while saying, "Get up, O Abū Turāb, get up O Abū Turāb".'

77 'The Prophet ﷺ travelled to Khaybar at the end of Muḥarram in the seventh year after the Migration. Khaybar is a large city with fortresses and agricultural fields, lying approximately 100 miles north of Medina in the direction of Syria.' Al-Būṭī, Muḥammad Saʿīd Ramaḍān, *Fiqh al-sīrah al-nabawiyyah*.

78 'On the authority of Salamah ibn ʿAmr ibn al-Akwaʿ that he said, "The Messenger of Allah ﷺ dispatched Abū Bakr al-Ṣiddīq ؓ with his war banner to some of the fortresses of Khaybar, where he fought and returned. He wasn't granted victory, in spite of having exerted himself. Then the next day he dispatched ʿUmar ؓ and he too fought and returned. He was not granted victory, while he too had exerted himself. Then the Messenger of Allah ﷺ said, 'Tomorrow I shall truly give the banner to a man who loves Allah and His Messenger. Allah shall grant victory at his hands, without him fleeing.' He [Ibn Isḥāq] stated, Salamah said, "So the Messenger of Allah ﷺ called ʿAlī ؓ, while he was nursing an eye ailment, so he ﷺ drizzled his saliva into his eye, then said, 'Take this banner and continue until Allah grants you success'." [...] On the authority of Abū Rāfiʿ, the freed-slave of the Messenger of Allah, who said, "We set out with ʿAlī ibn Abī Ṭālib when the Messenger of Allah ﷺ dispatched him with his banner. So when we approached the fortress, its people came out to him and he fought them. A Jewish man struck him and he lost the shield from his hand. Thus ʿAlī reached for a gate that

The hadiths establishing the love between him and the Prophet ﷺ are numerous, which dispenses with the need for any weak narrations, let alone any fabricated ones.

Furthermore, he ؓ had the utmost love for the caliphs that preceded him. On the day that ʿUthmān was besieged in his home, ʿAlī ؓ defended him, ordering his sons al-Ḥasan ؓ and al-Ḥusayn ؓ to do likewise. In fact, he would refute whoever gave preference to him over his predecessors, as narrated in many hadiths from him on this issue. An example of which is the hadith of ʿAlqamah al-Nakhaʿī, who said, "ʿAlī ؓ addressed us. Thus he [first] praised Allah and glorified Him then said, "Indeed, it has reached me that certain people consider me to be superior to Abū Bakr ؓ and ʿUmar ؓ! If I had them brought before me, I would surely have punished them for it. But I dislike to punish before the case is presented. So whoever says anything of the sort after this occasion, then [know] that he is a fabricator, and may he receive what fabricators receive! The best of people after the Messenger of Allah ﷺ is Abū Bakr ؓ, then ʿUmar ؓ, then after them we did what we did, and Allah will judge in that as He sees fit".'

It is narrated, on the authority of Zayd ibn Wahb, that Suwayd ibn Ghafalah entered upon ʿAlī ؓ during his reign as caliph and said, 'O Commander of the believers, I passed by a group of people who were mentioning Abū Bakr ؓ and ʿUmar ؓ in an unbefitting way.' So ʿAlī ؓ got up and ascended the pulpit and said, 'By the One Who split the grain

---

was at the [front of] the fortress, which he used to shield himself with. It remained in his hand while he was fighting until Allah granted him victory. Then he threw it down from his hand when he had finished. And you would have truly seen me with a group of seven alongside me – while I was the eighth – trying to turn over that gate and we weren't able to".' Ibn Hishām, Abū Muḥammad ʿAbd al-Malik al-Ḥimyarī, *al-Sīrah al-nabawiyyah*.

and created man, none loves those two except a virtuous believer and none has disdain for them except a wretched heretic. Thus to love them is a means to gain proximity [to Allah] and to have disdain for them is deviation. What is the state of people that they speak [ill] of the two brothers of the Messenger of Allah ﷺ – his two viziers, two companions, two leaders of Quraysh and two fathers of the Muslims? I dissociate myself from anyone who speaks ill of them and may he be punished for doing so.'

It is narrated that Saʿd ibn Abī Waqqāṣ ؓ said, 'I heard the Messenger of Allah ﷺ instruct ʿAlī ؓ after having left him behind during some of his military expeditions. So ʿAlī ؓ said to him ﷺ, "O Messenger of Allah, are you leaving me behind with the women and children?" The Messenger of Allah ﷺ replied, "Are you not pleased that you are to me as Hārun was to Mūsā, except that there is no prophethood after me?"'[79]

ʿAlī ؓ said, 'The unlettered Prophet ﷺ told me, "Only a believer loves you and only a hypocrite has disdain for you".'

This is what Ahl al-Sunnah[80] adhere to, loving ʿAlī and the Prophet's family ﷺ and supplicating for them in their prayers, gatherings of

---

[79] 'He – may Allah ennoble his face – was one of the scholars of divine gnosis and among the famous valiant heroes, whom he ﷺ gave the war banner to in many lands, just like he did on the day of Khaybar. On that day, he had carried the gate of its fortress on his back so that the Muslims could climb upon it and were victorious. After that they hauled it, and it required forty men to carry it. In a separate narration, ʿAlī used the gate of the fortress to shield himself and he did not release it from his hand while he was fighting until he was given victory by Allah.' Al-Maqdisī, al-ʿAllāmah Marʿī ibn Yūsuf al-Karamī al-Ḥanbalī, *Talkhīṣ awṣāf al-muṣṭafā ﷺ wa dhikr man baʿdahu min al-khulafā*.

[80] Referring to the Muslim orthodoxy, literally meaning the People of the Sunnah i.e. the way of the Prophet ﷺ and the Group of Muslims i.e. the Companions. The term has

remembrance and when alone in solitude. They seek blessings and good by invoking blessings and peace upon the Prophet's family ﷺ. May Allah be well pleased with them all and the Companions of the Messenger of Allah ﷺ.

---

a more specific usage when related to the field of theology, 'When the term Ahl al-Sunnah wa al-Jamāʿah is used, what is intended is the Ashʿarī's and the Māturīdī's. Al-Khiyālī in his marginalia upon *Sharḥ al-ʿaqā'id* stated, "The Ashʿarī's are Ahl al-Sunnah wa al-Jamāʿah. That is the widely-accepted view in the lands of Khorasan, Iraq, Greater Syria and most places. Whilst, in the lands of Transoxania, that expression is used to refer to the Māturīdī's – the followers of the Imam Abū Mansūr. Whilst between the two groups there is only difference over some issues such as *al-takwīn*".' Al-Zabīdī, Murtaḍā Muḥammad ibn Muḥammad al-Ḥusaynī, *Ittiḥāf al-sādah al-muttaqīn*.

PART FIVE

Notable Instances of the Companions' Love for the Messenger ﷺ

Abū Ayyūb al-Anṣārī's Hospitality ﵁

He is also known as Khālid ibn Zayd al-Najjārī from the clan of Banū al-Najjār, who are the maternal relatives of the Prophet ﷺ. Allah distinguished him by giving him the honour of accommodating the Prophet ﷺ in his home when he arrived in Medina. He displayed the utmost etiquette and affection for the Prophet ﷺ, and afforded him the very height of hospitality.

When the Prophet ﷺ stayed at Abū Ayyūb's home ﵁, he lived on the ground floor. The house had a second floor and it pained Abū Ayyūb ﵁ to see the Prophet ﷺ on the floor below. So he insisted that they swap, until the Prophet ﷺ explained that it was easier for him and the many people who would come to visit him.

Furthermore, he ﵁ would not eat until the Prophet ﷺ would eat. Thus he would prepare the food and send it to the Prophet ﷺ. Then when the bowl[81] was returned to him, he would look for the place where the Prophet's fingers had touched and then eat from where the Messenger ﷺ had eaten.

81 *Qaṣʿah*: a large wooden or copper bowl.

On one occasion, an earthenware jar containing water broke in Abū Ayyūb's house, which alarmed him and his wife ﵄. They rushed to get a wrap-around that they used as a blanket, and immediately began drying the water out of concern that some of it may seep away and inconvenience the Prophet ﷺ.

Sawād ibn al-Ghaziyyah ﵁ Kissing the Prophet's Abdomen ﷺ

While he ﷺ was straightening the rows of his Companions on the day of Badr, he had an arrow in his hand that he used to line up the people with. As he passed by Sawād ibn al-Ghaziyyah, he jabbed his stomach with it and said, 'Line up, O Sawād!' Sawād replied, 'O Messenger of Allah ﷺ, you hurt me even though Allah has sent you with truth and justice.' He ﷺ replied, 'Then take your retribution from me.' The Messenger of Allah ﷺ then uncovered his abdomen and said, 'Take your retribution!' Whereupon Sawād hugged him instead and kissed his stomach. So he ﷺ said, 'What caused you to do this, O Sawād?' He replied, 'The arrival of what you see before you (meaning war and death). So I wished that my final moment with you, be that my skin touches your skin.' Whereupon the Messenger of Allah ﷺ supplicated for him.

This occurred numerous times with other than Sawād ﵁, when they sought a way to kiss the abdomen of the Prophet ﷺ or the side of his noble body ﷺ. Likewise, instances of the Companions seeking blessings from the various parts of his body, that which he had touched or the remnants of the water of his ablution and the like, are extremely common. One such example among many, was mentioned earlier in relation to the Treaty of Ḥudaybiyyah.

Umm ʿAmmārah ﵁ Sacrificing Herself for the Prophet ﷺ

When the Muslims were attacked on the day of Uḥud[82], Umm ʿAmmārah ﵁ joined the Messenger ﷺ. She said, 'I stood fighting and defending him ﷺ with the sword and firing arrows with a longbow until I was finally beset with injury.'

82 'The expedition of Uḥud took place on a Saturday in mid-Shawwāl [3 AH]. He ﷺ mobilised his Companions and stationed them for the battle. The archers in the army were ordered to hold their position on the mountain by the Messenger ﷺ, who said, 'Remain in your position, whether we are victorious or defeated!' The Muslims started to gain such an overwhelming advantage that the majority of the archers on the mountain descended, as they perceived victory and thought the battle had ended. While in reality this was not the case. Consequently, the polytheists seized the opportunity presented by the Muslims' backs being exposed by the lack of protection from the archers. Khālid ibn al-Walīd bellowed at his cavalry and attacked the remaining archers, and the polytheists ended up killing them. They then attacked the Muslims from behind, and the Muslim lines crumbled. Quraysh – after their [initial] defeat – had fully regrouped and the enemy finally reached the Messenger of Allah ﷺ and pelted him with rocks, until he fell on his side, with his molar tooth broken and his lower lip and cheek wounded. Rumour spread that he had been killed while in fact he ﷺ, together with a group of Muslims had simply stood their ground. When the Muslims realised the Messenger of Allah ﷺ was still alive, they proceeded towards him and rallied around him. The battle took another turn, with the polytheists suffering defeat. Seventy Muslims were martyred, including the Chief of the Martyrs, Ḥamzah – the paternal uncle of the Messenger of Allah.' Al-Mālikī, Sayyid Muḥammad ibn ʿAlawī al-Ḥasanī, *Muhammad the best of creation: a glimpse of his blessed life.*

Umm Saʿd bint Saʿd ibn al-Rabīʿ, who narrates from her, stated, 'I saw a deep hollow wound on her shoulder. So I said to her, "Who inflicted this upon you?" She replied, "Ibn Qami'ah, may Allah humiliate him! When the people left the Messenger of Allah ﷺ, he came forward, saying, 'Show me where Muhammad is! May I not be saved if he is saved!' So I, Muṣʿab ibn ʿUmayr and some others who had stood their ground with the Messenger of Allah ﷺ, stood in his way. Then he struck me with a single blow, while I struck him numerous times in return. However, the enemy of Allah was wearing two suits of armour".'

Similar feats were performed by others, among them Qatādah ibn al-Nuʿmān ؓ, who said, 'On the day of Uḥud, I was guarding the face of the Messenger of Allah ﷺ with mine while Abū Dujānah Simāk ibn al-Kharashah ؓ was shielding the back of the Messenger of Allah ﷺ with his, until his back was laden with arrows.'

Abū Ṭalḥah ؓ also shielded the Messenger of Allah ﷺ with his body, as did others who stood their ground alongside the Prophet ﷺ, until the pagans were eventually compelled to cease fighting.

Seeking Solace with the Prophet ﷺ During Great Calamities

An example of this is the incident of a woman from the tribe of Banū Dīnār, which is well known among the scholars of the Prophetic biography and is supported by their chains of transmission. 'The Messenger of Allah ﷺ passed by a woman from Banū Dīnār, whose husband, brother and father were slain, while [fighting] alongside the Messenger of Allah ﷺ at Uḥud. When their death was announced to her, she said, "What has happened to the Messenger of Allah ﷺ?" They replied, "He is well [...] with Allah's praise, he is as you would like." She said, "Show him to me, so that I may see him".' The narrator states, 'So he was pointed out to her, and when she could see him, she said, "Every calamity after you is trivial".'

Her immense tribulation was alleviated when she found the Prophet ﷺ to be safe and well. May Allah be pleased with her!

A further example of the Companions gaining solace from the Prophet ﷺ is Saʿd ibn al-Rabīʿ, a member of the Anṣār. He was heavily wounded on the day of Uḥud, barely alive, with seventy wounds from the piercing of spears, arrows and blows from swords. An envoy from the Messenger of Allah ﷺ came with the duty of conveying the Messenger's greetings of peace and to find out about his condition. He replied, 'Peace be upon the Messenger of Allah ﷺ and may peace be upon you. Say to him, "O Messenger of Allah ﷺ, I find myself to have found the breeze of paradise." And say to my people, the Anṣār, "You have no excuse with Allah from the Messenger of Allah ﷺ being reached [by the enemy], so long as you can still bat an eyelid".' And with that his soul passed on, may Allah be pleased with him.

Likewise we see the case of Anas ibn al-Naḍr ﷺ, the paternal uncle of Anas ibn Mālik ﷺ, who said to a visitor, 'Say to my people, the Anṣār, "You have no excuse with Allah from the Messenger of Allah ﷺ being reached [by the enemy], so long as you have an eyelid that flickers".' There are many other statements similar to this from the Companions – may Allah be pleased with them.

ʿAmr ibn al-ʿĀṣ ﷺ would say, 'There is no one more beloved to me than the Messenger of Allah ﷺ, nor anyone more majestic in my sight than he. Out of reverence for him, I was not able to look at him properly, to the extent that if it was said, "Describe him," I would not be able to do so.'

Thamāmah ibn al-Uthāl ﷺ, who was the chief of al-Yamāmah[83], was at war with Islam. Yet when Islam entered his heart, he came to the Prophet ﷺ and said, 'I bear witness that there is no god besides Allah, and I bear

83 Yamāmah: an ancient region lying to the east of the plateau of Najd in modern-day Saudi Arabia, named after the ancient village of Jaww al-Yamāmah. It was the central location of the Apostasy (Riddah) Wars that occurred during the caliphate of Abū Bakr ﷺ.

witness that Muhammad ﷺ is His Slave and Messenger. O Muhammad, by Allah, there was no face on earth more detestable to me than your face, yet now your face has become the most beloved of all faces to me. By Allah, there was not a single religion more detestable to me than your religion, yet now your religion has become the most beloved of all religions to me. By Allah, there was no city more detestable to me than your city, yet your city has now become more beloved to me than all cities.'

Yearning for the Messenger of Allah ﷺ

Part of the Companions' ؓ love for the Prophet ﷺ was their yearning for him. As has been mentioned previously, Bilāl ؓ said on his deathbed, 'O what joy! Tomorrow I shall meet the loved ones – Muhammad ﷺ and his Companions.'

'Thawbān ؓ – the freed slave of the Messenger ﷺ – came to the Messenger of Allah ﷺ and said, "O Messenger of Allah ﷺ, truly you are more beloved to me than my family and my wealth. Whenever I remember you, I cannot wait patiently until I come and see you. I remembered your death and my death, and realised that when you enter paradise you will be raised up alongside the prophets, and if I were to enter it, I will not see you".'

So Allah Most High revealed, 'And whoever obeys Allah and the Messenger, they will be with the ones upon whom Allah has bestowed favour – among the prophets, the truthful, the martyrs and the righteous. And excellent are they as companions!'[84] Whereupon, he ﷺ summoned him and recited the verse over him.

---

84 Qur'an 4:69.

Examples of this sort are many, as their entire lives were filled with the love of the Prophet ﷺ. Indeed the Prophetic era is rich with events of striving with one's soul and all things precious, longing for him ﷺ and obedience to him, irrespective of how much it opposed their own desires.

Then after his noble life, they carried on striving despite their small number and lack of infrastructure. Consequently, they flooded nations with a love that radiated from their conduct, as a result of their esteem for the Messenger of Allah ﷺ, his noble character traits, honour and sacrifices. Such was the effect, that their way of life became a cause for hearts to open up and for the Companions to be preferred over the natives of lands that were conquered, whether they were men of faith or men of the world. This is of no surprise, as they were the best of all generations.[85] They were emulated by the Successors and those after them. It was from the Companions that they had learnt noble character traits and virtues, through their actions and good conduct, prior to the Companions teaching them through words and narrations.

Exhaustive research is a lengthy process. It requires investigating all of the prophetic biography, then the historical accounts of the Companions – and no topic has been written about more than that – and then the entire history of Islam. We have presented to you some examples here of the Companions' love for the beloved Messenger ﷺ, so emulate them, for they are the intermediaries between him ﷺ and the rest of humanity that followed.

---

85 Al-Tirmidhī relates that the Messenger of Allah ﷺ said, 'The best of generations is my generation, then those that follow them, then those that follow them.'

PART SIX

CONCLUSION

The Hallmarks of True Love for the Messenger ﷺ

Before concluding, we will remind you of three hallmarks that indicate one's love of the Prophet ﷺ:

1. Love for the members of his household ﷺ. This includes his wives[86] – the Mothers of the believers[87] – his progeny and all his relatives, because of His Most High's Words, 'Allah only intends to remove from you the impurity [of sin], O people of the [Prophet's] household, and to purify you with complete purification.'[88] Allah's address prior

86 'On the authority of Hind ibn Hind Abī Hālah from his father, that the Messenger of Allah ﷺ said, "Allah has refused me from [both] marrying or giving in marriage except for the people of heaven".' Al-Ṣāliḥī, Shams al-Dīn Muḥammad ibn Yūsuf al-Dimashqī al-Shāfiʿī, *Azwāj al-nabī* ﷺ.

87 The title conferred to the wives of the Prophet ﷺ in the Qur'an (33:6), 'Allah Most High stated, "and his wives are their mothers." Meaning mothers unto the Believers in terms of their great importance and deference afforded to them, as well as the impermissibility of ever marrying them. As such, they are like mothers.' Al-Ṣāliḥī, Shams al-Dīn Muḥammad ibn Yūsuf al-Dimashqī al-Shāfiʿī, *Azwāj al-nabī* ﷺ.

88 Qur'an 33:33.

to this verse and directly after it is to the Mothers of the believers – thus their inclusion in this verse is necessary.

Love of the Household of the Prophet is something inherent in every Muslim and particularly for the people of Ahl al-Sunnah wa al-Jamāʿah as it is a necessary consequence of love for the Prophet ﷺ. He ﷺ said, 'Love Allah because He nourishes you from His Blessings, and love me because of your love for Allah, and love my family because of your love for me.'

2. Love for his Companions ﷵ. For they were the supporters of the Messenger of Allah ﷺ, those that conveyed the religion from him ﷺ and his ambassadors to the world. The Qur'anic verses and hadiths regarding their virtue are many, such as His Words Most High, 'You are the best nation brought forth for mankind';[89] 'Muhammad is the Messenger of Allah and those with him are unyielding against the disbelievers, merciful between themselves';[90] 'Allah was well-pleased with the believers when they swore allegiance to you under the tree';[91] and many other such examples. Similarly, the hadiths on this matter are numerous too. Among them is the mass-transmitted hadith, 'The best of mankind is my generation...' and his saying ﷺ, in an agreed-upon narration, 'Do not insult my Companions, for if one of you were to give in charity the equivalent of [Mount] Uḥud in gold it would not equate to a handful in charity from one of them, and not even half of it.'

89 Qur'an 3:110.
90 Qur'an 48:29.
91 Qur'an 48:18.

3. Assessing one's love for him ﷺ within oneself. Which is to present oneself with the choice between being deprived of a certain desire or being deprived of seeing the Prophet ﷺ if it was an option. If the loss of seeing him ﷺ – were it possible for one – is more difficult to bear than the loss of a desire, then one is characterised as having greater love for the Messenger of Allah ﷺ. Otherwise, one is not. Likewise, is the case regarding the defence of the Sunnah of the Prophet ﷺ and his shariah and giving sincere counsel.

Concluding Remarks

We conclude with the following hadith and the supplication contained therein, which is inscribed with love. On the authority of Muʿādh ibn Jabal ﷺ, who said the Messenger of Allah ﷺ took his hand one day then said, 'O Muʿādh, by Allah, I truly love you!' So Muʿādh replied, 'May my mother and father be ransom for you. By Allah I love you too!' He ﷺ said, 'I enjoin you, O Muʿādh, not to forget to say at the end of each prayer, "O Allah, assist me to remember You, show gratitude to You and to worship You with excellence".'

And we say, 'O Allah, we ask You for Your love and the love of Your Prophet, our master Muhammad ﷺ, and that You make the love of You and Your Prophet ﷺ more beloved to us than our wealth, offspring, fathers, mothers and cool water at the point of thirst. O Allah! Āmīn.'

May Allah bless our master Muhammad ﷺ, his family and his Companions, and grant them peace, and may peace be upon the Messengers, and all praise belongs to the Lord of the Worlds.

Written by one needy of his Lord's pardon, Nūr al-Dīn ʿItr
Servant to the Qur'an, hadith and their sciences.